NICK SHAW

12 Month Millionaire: Build, Grow and Thrive

Copyright © 2024 by Nick Shaw

All rights reserved. No part of this publication may be reproduced, stored or transmitted in any form or by any means, electronic, mechanical, photocopying, recording, scanning, or otherwise without written permission from the publisher. It is illegal to copy this book, post it to a website, or distribute it by any other means without permission.

First edition

This book was professionally typeset on Reedsy.
Find out more at reedsy.com

Contents

Introduction	1
Chapter 1: Setting the Foundation	5
Defining Your Why	5
Establishing Your Vision	8
Chapter 2: Identifying Your Winning Product Idea	11
Market Research Techniques	11
Product Selection Criteria	14
Chapter 3: Securing Funding	18
Bootstrapping	18
Attracting Investors	22
Chapter 4: The Grind (Months 0-4)	25
Finding Your Target Customers	25
Crafting an Irresistible Offer	28
Launching Your Product	31
Chapter 5: First Sales Tactics	34
Creating Urgency and Scarcity	34
Leveraging Early Adopters	37
Chapter 6: Streamlining Operations	40
Building Efficient Systems	40
Managing Inventory	43
Chapter 7: The Growth (Months 5-8)	46
Advertising on a Budget	46
Scaling Your Marketing Efforts	49
Chapter 8: Achieving 25 Sales Per Day	53
Optimizing Conversion Rates	53
Retargeting Strategies	56

Chapter 9: Expanding Your Reach	59
Influencer Partnerships	59
Social Media Marketing	62
Chapter 10: Enhancing Customer Experience	65
Feedback Loops	65
Building Customer Loyalty	69
Chapter 11: Financial Management	72
Budgeting for Growth	72
Cash Flow Management	75
Chapter 12: The Gold (Months 9-12)	79
Establishing a Product Series	79
Diversifying Your Offerings	82
Chapter 13: Sustaining 100 Sales Per Day	86
Advanced Sales Techniques	86
Loyalty Programs	89
Chapter 14: Automating Your Business	93
Leveraging Technology	93
Outsourcing Tasks	97
Chapter 15: Advanced Marketing Strategies	100
Email Marketing	100
Content Marketing	103
Chapter 16: Building a Brand	107
Crafting Your Brand Story	107
Consistent Brand Messaging	110
Chapter 17: Analyzing Metrics	113
Key Performance Indicators (KPIs)	113
Data-Driven Decisions	115
Chapter 18: Optimizing Profit Margins	119
Cost Reduction Strategies	119
Increasing Average Order Value	122
Chapter 19: Continuous Improvement	126
Implementing Feedback	126
Iterative Testing	129

Chapter 20: Crisis Management	133
Navigating Economic Downturns	133
Handling Negative Feedback	135
Chapter 21: Long-term Sustainability	139
Building a Community	139
Planning for the Future	142
Chapter 22: Networking and Mentorship	145
Finding Mentors	145
Building Your Network	148
Chapter 23: Legal and Compliance	151
Understanding Regulations	151
Intellectual Property Protection	154
Chapter 24: Innovation and Evolution	157
Staying Ahead of Trends	157
Adapting to Market Changes	160
Chapter 25: Preparing For Exits	163
Evaluating Exit Strategies	163
Preparing for Sale or IPO	166
Conclusion	170
Appendix	173
Appendix A: Appendix	173
Resource List	173
Glossary	176
Further Reading	178

Introduction

Welcome to the first step of your journey toward a million-dollar milestone. Whether you're an entrepreneur just starting out, a seasoned business owner eager for the next big leap, or someone juggling kids and daily chores while dreaming of financial freedom, this book is for you. It doesn't matter where you're beginning from; the principles outlined here are universal and have been proven by countless successful individuals.

Imagine this: one year from now, you look back and see a thriving business that generates substantial revenue, affords you the lifestyle you crave, and allows you to impact others positively. This vision is not a pipe dream. It's a plan—a clear, structured path we're about to embark on together. This one-year plan will guide you through three pivotal stages to your first $1 million. It's a journey built on dedication, strategic thinking, and relentless execution.

Why focus on $1 million? It's a psychologically salient figure, an aspirational metric that has stood the test of time. It signifies more than just money—it represents success, stability, and a level of achievement that can elevate your life in myriad ways. But before we dive into the blueprint, let's understand the foundational elements that will be critical to your success.

We start with understanding your "why." What drives you? What inspires you to wake up every morning and give it your all? This journey demands more than just wishful thinking; it demands a robust and unwavering motivation that will keep you going despite the inevitable challenges. Your "why" is your anchor. Without it, even the best strategies will flounder.

In addition to your "why," establishing your vision is equally crucial. You have to see it to achieve it. A clear vision provides direction, keeping you focused and aligned with your ultimate goal. It shapes your decisions, fuels your determination, and transforms obstacles into stepping stones. Once you've articulated your vision, you'll find that every action you take brings you one step closer to that million-dollar mark.

Next up is identifying your winning product idea. You can't vend just any product and expect success; it needs to be something that resonates with your target audience and solves a genuine problem. We'll delve into market research techniques to uncover lucrative opportunities and select products with the highest potential for success. This isn't about guessing; it's about making informed, data-driven choices.

Securing funding is essential. While bootstrapping can be a viable option for some, attracting investors might be necessary for those requiring significant upfront capital. We'll discuss different funding avenues, helping you determine the optimal strategy for your specific circumstances. Money should never be a barrier to innovation and progress; rather, it should be a tool that helps you achieve your goals.

The grind—those first four months where you're laying the groundwork—is where the magic begins. You'll find yourself immersed in finding your target customers, crafting irresistible offers, and launching your product with a bang. It's intense, unglamorous work, but it's also incredibly rewarding. This is where you begin transforming your vision into reality, one step at a time.

After the initial grind, we'll focus on first sales tactics. Creating urgency and scarcity, leveraging early adopters, and mastering the art of the initial push are essential. Your first sales are a critical milestone that validates your idea and provides the momentum needed to scale. It's about generating buzz, creating demand, and getting your product into the hands of your customers.

Streamlining operations allows you to build a sustainable business. Efficient systems and inventory management are vital for ensuring smooth and cost-effective operations. You'll learn how to optimize these processes, saving time and resources that can then be reinvested into growth areas.

INTRODUCTION

As you transition into the growth phase (months 5-8), scaling your marketing efforts and advertising on a budget become pivotal. It's not just about expansion but smart expansion. You'll learn to balance cost-effectiveness with reach, maximizing your impact without breaking the bank.

Then, achieving 25 sales per day becomes the next focused milestone. To hit this, we'll explore optimizing conversion rates and retargeting strategies that keep your base engaged and continually bring in new customers. Every aspect of your sales funnel will be fine-tuned to drive consistent, scalable sales.

As your business grows, expanding your reach through influencer partnerships and robust social media marketing strategies will be key. These methods amplify your message and broaden your audience, ensuring that your product reaches more potential customers than ever before.

Enhancing customer experience isn't just a nicety; it's a necessity. Building strong feedback loops and cultivating customer loyalty can make or break your long-term success. Happy customers are repeat customers, and they're also your best advocates.

Financial management is often the backdrop of any successful venture. You'll master budgeting for growth and managing cash flow to ensure that your business remains in the green as you expand. Money management is about precision and foresight, enabling you to invest wisely and sustainably.

In the last quarter (months 9-12), the focus turns to establishing a product series and diversifying your offerings to cater to broader market needs. Variety and innovation keep your brand relevant and appealing, ensuring continued growth and customer retention.

Sustaining 100 sales per day will be the climax of this journey. Advanced sales techniques and loyalty programs will secure your position in the market. This consistent performance aligns with long-term growth and stability, building a legacy that lasts.

Automation and streamlining through technology set the stage for operating a scalable, efficient business. Outsourcing tasks and leveraging tech will free up your time for strategic planning and further growth. Smart automation keeps your business running smoothly, even as your responsibilities evolve.

With your base solidly established, advanced marketing strategies like email and content marketing will help maintain and accelerate growth. These are tools that nurture customer relationships and create ongoing engagement, turning casual buyers into brand champions.

Brand-building is the emotional core of your business. Crafting your brand story and maintaining consistent messaging will differentiate you in a crowded market. Your brand is your identity, and a strong one builds trust and loyalty with your audience.

Analyzing metrics ensures that every decision is data-driven. Focusing on key performance indicators will inform your strategies and keep you on the right path. Data doesn't lie; it guides you towards continuous improvement and strategic decision-making.

Optimizing profit margins involves both cost reduction and increasing the average order value. It's about making every sale as profitable as possible without compromising quality or customer satisfaction. Efficiency paired with profitability is the key to long-term success.

Continuous improvement is a mindset. Implementing feedback and iterative testing ensures your business remains adaptable and resilient. This agility allows you to respond to changes and stay ahead of trends, ensuring your continued relevance and success.

Crisis management is unavoidable. Navigating economic downturns and handling negative feedback with grace and efficiency can turn challenges into opportunities. How you manage crises often defines your business's resilience and longevity.

Long-term sustainability involves building a community and planning for the future. This is about more than just business; it's about creating a lasting impact and ensuring your venture benefits others while ensuring your

Chapter 1: Setting the Foundation

Embarking on the journey to your first $1 million requires a solid foundation, grounded in both your personal drive and clear vision. Start by defining your "why" – that fundamental reason that propels you out of bed each morning and keeps you going when times get tough. This intrinsic motivation isn't just a feel-good exercise; it's the backbone that will anchor you through the inevitable ebbs and flows of entrepreneurial life. Next, move on to establishing your vision. This isn't about grandiose dreams; it's about articulating a clear, achievable picture of where you want your business to go. When your "why" aligns seamlessly with a well-defined vision, you're not just setting a foundation; you're crafting a roadmap for success. Remember, this initial groundwork isn't a one-time activity but a living, breathing part of your journey, evolving right alongside you and your enterprise. Ready to build your empire? Then let's lay that cornerstone together, ensuring every decision, every move, and every pivot is deeply rooted in purpose and clarity.

Defining Your Why

In any journey, knowing why you're setting off in the first place is crucial. When it comes to building a successful business, your "why" is your compass, guiding you through the highs and lows. It provides clarity, motivation, and a sense of purpose. Without a strong "why," even the most promising ventures can falter.

So, why define your why? Simply put, it's what keeps you grounded. In the entrepreneurial world, challenges are a guarantee. There will be moments you'll question your path, face failures, and wonder if it's all worth it. Your "why" will be the anchor that holds you steady, helping you navigate through difficult periods with resilience and grace.

Think about some of the most successful entrepreneurs out there; they didn't start their businesses for money alone. They had a deeper reason, often emotional and compelling, driving them forward. Your "why" needs to be something that resonates deeply with you, something that's unshakeable no matter the circumstances.

Now, let's talk about finding your why. Start by asking yourself some probing questions. What excites you? What problem do you want to solve in the world? Why are you passionate about this particular venture? Maybe you've experienced a personal challenge that you believe others face as well. Maybe it's about creating a legacy for your family. Whatever it is, it needs to be deeply personal.

One effective way to uncover your why is to think about the impact you want to have. Picture the transformation you'll bring about, not just for yourself but for others. How will your product or service change lives? Create a vivid mental image of your success story, of happy customers, and of the difference you're making.

Once you've identified your why, write it down. Make it tangible by putting it on paper. Hang it somewhere you can see daily as a constant reminder of why you started this journey in the first place. It's your personal mission statement, encapsulating your goals and values. It's more than just motivation; it's your reason for being in business.

Your why isn't static. As your business grows and evolves, your motivations might shift. That's perfectly normal. What's important is regularly revisiting your why and ensuring it still aligns with your vision and goals. Flexibility in your mission can be a strong asset as long as the core motivation inspires you.

Interestingly, your why can also be a powerful tool when attracting a team or investors. People are drawn to purpose-driven businesses. They're more likely to join your mission if they understand and resonate with your why.

When you can clearly articulate your purpose, you create a sense of shared vision and commitment.

Let's delve into a few examples. Consider a single parent who's passionate about creating educational toys because they struggled to find quality options for their children. Their why is straightforward—they want to make life easier for other parents while fostering their children's development. Or take a tech enthusiast who saw a gap in accessibility tools for people with disabilities. They're driven by a desire to make technology inclusive for everyone.

Does your why need to be grandiose? Absolutely not. It could be as simple as wanting financial freedom or setting a positive example for your children. The magnitude of the why doesn't matter, but the depth of your conviction does. If you truly believe in why you will find the drive to overcome any obstacle.

Once you've defined your why, share it. Communicate it through your branding, your pitch deck, and your marketing efforts. Your why should be evident in every interaction and every piece of content you create. It's not just an internal compass but also a tool to connect with your audience on a deeper level.

On tough days, and there will be many, revisiting your why can provide much-needed motivation. When faced with setbacks, it's easy to get discouraged. But when you remember the bigger picture and the reason behind your hustle, it becomes easier to persevere. Your why will fuel your resilience.

Balancing the demands of building a business while maintaining that sense of purpose can be challenging. It's easy to get caught up in the day-to-day tasks and lose sight of your mission. Regularly schedule a time for reflection. Assess whether you're still aligned with your why and if you're staying true to your mission. This practice will keep you focused and grounded.

In summary, defining your why is a foundational step in your entrepreneurial journey. It's the driving force that propels you forward, offering clarity and direction. Whether you're aiming to make a million dollars, create a groundbreaking product, or leave a lasting legacy, your why is what will keep you steadfast in your mission. Embrace it, nurture it, and let it guide you every step of the way.

Next, we'll dive into how to establish a vision that's aligned with your why, setting the stage for a strategic and impactful journey toward your first million dollars.

Establishing Your Vision

As we continue to set the foundation of your entrepreneurial journey, it's crucial to take a moment to define what success looks like for you. Establishing your vision is not just a superficial exercise; it's about mapping out a clear, compelling destination that will guide every decision and action you take moving forward. Think of your vision as your North Star, the beacon that keeps you aligned with your ultimate goals even when life throws its inevitable curveballs.

First, let's dive into the core of what a vision statement is. A well-crafted vision statement encapsulates your long-term aspirations and the ultimate impact you aim to make. It should be vivid enough that when you read it, you feel a rush of excitement and purpose. A strong vision doesn't just focus on financial success—it embodies your values, passions, and the broader contribution you wish to make to society. To illustrate this, think about companies like Apple or Tesla; their vision statements go beyond selling products—they aim to change the world as we know it.

Begin by reflecting on the why behind your business idea. What drives you to wake up early and stay up late, continually pushing through the obstacles that come your way? Your vision should be an extension of this powerful 'why'. Consider not just what you want to achieve, but why it matters to you and to the world at large. When your vision aligns with something you deeply care about, it becomes infinitely easier to stay motivated, even during tough times.

Once you have a general idea of what you want your business to achieve, it's time to get specific. Take the time to jot down your thoughts—write freely without worrying about structure or grammar. This brainstorming phase is about capturing the essence of your aspirations. Afterwards, refine your thoughts into a clear, concise vision statement. Remember, less is more. Aim for a statement that's easy to remember and articulate, yet rich with meaning.

CHAPTER 1: SETTING THE FOUNDATION

For example, a vision statement like "To revolutionize the consumer electronics industry by making innovative technology accessible to everyone," is impactful and clear. It tells your team, investors, and customers exactly what you aim to accomplish and sets the stage for the strategic decisions you'll make along the way.

Another critical component of establishing your vision is understanding its role in decision-making. Your vision acts as a filter through which all major business decisions should pass. If an opportunity or strategy doesn't align with your vision, it becomes easier to set it aside and focus on what truly matters. This clarity can save you time, energy, and resources by preventing you from chasing after every shiny object that comes your way.

A compelling vision also serves as a rallying cry for your team. As you begin to hire and grow, you'll find that a shared vision fosters cohesion and a sense of purpose among your employees. When your team members understand and buy into the vision, they're more likely to put in the extra effort and collaborate effectively to achieve it. Your vision should be a key component of your onboarding process, ensuring that every new hire is aligned from day one.

Beyond your internal team, a well-communicated vision can also build trust and loyalty among your customers. In today's market, consumers are increasingly drawn to brands that share their values and demonstrate a commitment to something greater than profit. Don't shy away from sharing your vision in your marketing materials, website, and social media channels. Authenticity resonates, and when customers feel that they're part of something meaningful, they're more likely to become loyal advocates for your brand.

It's important to recognize that your vision is not set in stone. As you grow and your business evolves, your vision may need to adapt. Regularly revisiting your vision statement ensures it remains relevant and inspiring. Don't resist tweaking it as needed; the core essence should remain the same, but the specifics can shift to reflect new insights, market changes, or personal growth.

This iterative process of refining your vision is invaluable. Set aside time every six months or annually to review and reflect on it. Gather input from your team and even your customers to ensure your vision still resonates and inspires. By doing so, you not only keep the vision alive but also empower yourself and your team to stay aligned and focused on what truly matters.

Let's circle back to our initial brainstorming exercise. Now that you've refined your personal vision, consider how it integrates with your business strategy. Your vision should have actionable components. Break it down into long-term goals and milestones that will help you track progress. Having these tangible benchmarks allows you to measure your advancement and celebrate victories along the way, making the journey toward your vision not only purposeful but also rewarding.

Think of your vision as a living entity—it should grow and evolve just as you and your business do. Adaptability is key to maintaining a vision that remains meaningful and relevant. Alongside your vision statement, develop a vision board or digital equivalent. Populate it with images, quotes, and other elements that represent the future you're working towards. This visual representation can be a powerful tool to keep your aspirations front and center, serving as a daily reminder of your ultimate goals.

Let's wrap up this section with a call to action. Right now, set aside a dedicated hour in your calendar to brainstorm, jot down, and refine your vision. This isn't just a one-time activity but a pivotal step that will inform every decision you make from here on out. Embrace this process with open-mindedness and creativity; your vision is a reflection of your dreams, potential, and the legacy you intend to build. Establish it with care and watch as it becomes the cornerstone of your entrepreneurial journey to that coveted first million dollars.

Chapter 2: Identifying Your Winning Product Idea

Jumping from a mere concept to a thriving business starts with identifying your winning product idea. This isn't just about brainstorming what's cool or trendy—it's about tapping into a market need that aligns with your passion and expertise. Combine thorough market research with instinct to pinpoint an idea that not only excites you but also has genuine demand. The sweet spot is where your interests and market opportunities converge. Your winning product idea will be the anchor for everything that follows, setting the stage for innovation, customer satisfaction, and ultimately, financial success. Get ready to turn your insights into an exciting venture that can withstand the test of time and scale for growth.

Market Research Techniques

When it comes to identifying your winning product idea, the importance of market research can't be overstated. Picture this—it's the solid ground upon which you'll build your empire. The stronger your foundation, the higher you can soar. To start, let's break down the essential market research techniques that will help you pinpoint a product idea that resonates with your target audience and has money-making potential.

The first step in market research is to understand your potential customers. You need to know who they are, what they want, and where they hang out. This is often referred to as customer profiling. Build out a detailed persona for your ideal customer. Ask yourself: What are their pain points? What needs are not being met by current products? Engage with them directly through surveys, questionnaires, and even one-on-one interviews to gather this information.

Online tools can be an invaluable resource for direct feedback. Platforms like Google Forms, Typeform, and SurveyMonkey can streamline the process of collecting and analyzing data. Social media also offers countless opportunities to interact with potential customers. By joining relevant groups on platforms like Facebook or LinkedIn, you can gain insights and initiate discussions to validate your product ideas.

Next up is competitor analysis. Before you dive headfirst into a new product idea, you should know who your competitors are and what they're offering. Identify your top five competitors and take a close look at their best-selling products. What are the key features? What are the price points? What kind of customer reviews do they receive? Analyzing competitors isn't about copying them—it's about finding gaps and opportunities where your product can stand out.

Use tools like SEMrush, Ahrefs, and Moz to understand the competitive landscape better. These platforms give you insights into your competitors' online presence, including keywords they're targeting, backlinks, and even their advertising strategies. If you understand what's already working in your market, you're a step closer to finding your own edge.

Another valuable technique is trend analysis. Keeping an eye on emerging trends can give you foresight into what might be the "next big thing." Websites like Google Trends, Trend Hunter, and even Pinterest can show you what's gaining traction. Look for patterns or sudden spikes in interest—these could be signals that a particular product or niche is on the rise.

Attending industry-specific conferences, webinars, and trade shows can also provide rich insights. Networking with industry experts, potential customers, and other entrepreneurs could spark new ideas or validate existing ones. Additionally, these events often showcase the latest innovations and upcoming trends within specific markets, giving you a competitive edge.

Focus groups are another classic research technique that remains effective.

CHAPTER 2: IDENTIFYING YOUR WINNING PRODUCT IDEA

Bringing together a small group of potential customers to discuss your product idea can offer deep insights into consumer opinions and behaviors. The qualitative feedback gained from focus groups is invaluable for understanding the emotional and rational responses to your product.

Let's not forget about secondary research—information that's already out there for you to analyze. This includes market reports, industry journals, and studies conducted by research firms. Sources like IBISWorld, Statista, and Nielsen compile extensive data that can provide insights into market size, growth rates, and consumer behavior. This established information acts as a robust backbone for your hypothesis.

Customer journey mapping is another key technique. Understand deeply how potential customers discover, evaluate, and purchase products in your niche. By optimizing every stage of this journey—from awareness to decision—you can tailor your product to exceed expectations at each touchpoint, thereby increasing your chances of market success.

It's also a good idea to utilize A/B testing during the initial stages of your product development. Create multiple variations of your product idea, and test them with small segments of your target market. Collect data on which version performs better in terms of engagement, interest, or willingness to buy. This iterative process helps fine-tune your product to align closely with market demands.

Mentioning pre-orders and crowdfunding here as research techniques is worth noting. Platforms like Kickstarter and Indiegogo allow you to gauge interest in your product before it's even produced. Not only can this validate your idea, but you can also secure initial funding and build a community of early adopters who are invested in your success from the get-go.

The rich amounts of data you gather through these diverse methods should be systematically analyzed. Use software like Tableau or Google Data Studio to visualize data sets, making it easier to spot trends or insights that might not be obvious at first glance. Visualization tools can help transform raw data into actionable insights.

Don't underestimate the power of pilot launches and test markets. Before going all-in, consider launching your product in a smaller, controlled environment. This allows you to gather real-world feedback and make any necessary tweaks. A pilot launch can also provide a glimpse into how your product will perform on a larger scale, reducing the risk of failure when you officially go to market.

Podcasting and influencer collaborations serve as modern arenas for gauging public interest. Hosting or appearing on podcasts that align with your industry can help you reach and engage with an audience, gathering feedback in the process. Partnering with influencers provides another layer of validation, as their followers' reactions to your product give you further insight into market readiness.

Finally, stay adaptable and iterative. Market research isn't a one-and-done task. It requires continuous refinement and adaptation based on the feedback and data you collect. Stay connected with your audience through engagement strategies like newsletters, social media interaction, and post-purchase surveys.

By integrating these market research techniques into your product ideation process, you're not just taking stabs in the dark. You're crafting a product grounded in real-world data and needs—one that's primed to conquer any market. Whether you're a seasoned entrepreneur or just starting, this thorough approach lays down the stepping stones on your journey to the first million.

Product Selection Criteria

When it comes to selecting your winning product idea, there are numerous factors you need to consider to ensure you've chosen a category or niche with potential for success. This section will break down the critical elements you should evaluate when identifying which products will drive you towards that first million.

First and foremost, understanding market demand is crucial. You can have the greatest product idea, but if there's no demand, you're setting yourself up for failure. Start by examining current trends. Are there rising searches or increasing chatter on social media about certain products? Tools like Google

CHAPTER 2: IDENTIFYING YOUR WINNING PRODUCT IDEA

Trends and various keyword research tools can offer invaluable insights into what consumers are currently looking for. Look for products that not only have high search volumes but also show an upward trend: a sign that the product is gaining popularity, not just a fleeting fad.

Next, consider the problem-solving aspect of your product. Does it solve a real pain point or fulfill a significant need for your target audience? Products that address common issues tend to perform better in the market because they offer tangible value. Often, people are willing to pay a premium for solutions that make their lives easier or more enjoyable. Being clear about the problem your product solves can also help you craft compelling marketing messages that resonate with potential buyers.

Don't forget to evaluate the competition. A little bit of competition is a good sign—it shows there's demand—but too much can make it harder to stand out. Analyze what your competitors are doing right and where they might be lacking. Is there a gap in the market that you can fill? Perhaps your competitors have longer delivery times, and you can win customers over by offering faster shipping. Maybe their customer service is lacking, and you can differentiate by providing exceptional support. By identifying these gaps, you can position your product uniquely and gain an edge over others in the market.

The scalability of your product is another key factor. Will you be able to source and manufacture your product in larger quantities as your business grows? Is the supply chain reliable? Products that are easy to scale will save you a lot of headaches down the road and make the journey towards that million much smoother. Avoid categories with complex logistics or heavy reliance on scarce materials unless you're confident in the reliability of your supply chains.

Pricing and profit margins should also be on top of your mind. You need to find a sweet spot where your product is affordable for your target audience but still leaves you with a healthy profit margin. Do some market research to understand what price points are acceptable for your product category. Calculate your costs meticulously, factoring in not just the manufacturing but also your marketing, shipping, and any other expenses. High perceived value products often allow for better margins, so think about how you can position your product to appear premium without breaking the bank for production.

Consider the product lifecycle as well. Ideally, you want a product that will not only sell well initially but also have long-term potential. Consumable items or products with frequent repeat purchases are golden in this regard. However, even if your product is not consumable, think about how you can expand your offerings around it. Offering complementary products can keep customers coming back and increase your overall revenue per customer.

One often-overlooked aspect is the regulatory environment. Some products come with heavy compliance requirements, which can be a significant barrier for a small business. Make sure you understand any regulations or standards applicable to your product category. Ignoring these can lead to costly legal issues down the road, which could drain your resources and halt your momentum.

Let's not forget customer feedback. While it's important to go into your product selection with a clear direction, remember to be flexible and adjust based on what your customers are telling you. Initial feedback can be a goldmine for insights on how to further refine your product. Engage with your early customers, ask for their opinions, and be prepared to make improvements. This can turn them into loyal advocates who promote your product through word-of-mouth.

The branding potential of a product is also something to consider. In a saturated market, strong branding can set you apart from the competition. Does your product allow for a unique and engaging brand story? Can you create an emotional connection with your customers through your branding efforts? Products that allow for strong branding often perform better because they build a loyal customer base that transcends individual purchases.

Lastly, but equally important, consider your own passion and interest in the product. Building a business is a long and challenging journey, and your enthusiasm for your product will be crucial in keeping you motivated. Make sure you're genuinely interested in the product you're planning to sell. Your passion will come through in your marketing efforts, customer interactions, and overall business ethos, making a significant difference in your success.

In conclusion, selecting the right product involves a careful balance of market research, competitive analysis, scalability, pricing, regulatory compliance, and personal passion. Pay close attention to these criteria to ensure you're choosing a product with strong potential for success. By combining a thorough and strategic approach with a real passion for what you're selling, you're setting yourself up for a winning product idea that will pave the way to your first $1 million.

Chapter 3: Securing Funding

Securing funding is the lifeblood of any budding entrepreneurial venture. Whether you choose to bootstrap your business by relying on personal savings and revenue, or decide to attract investors eager to support your vision, understanding your options and choosing the right path is crucial. It's about balancing risk and reward, and sometimes it means wearing many hats or sipping more than a few late-night coffees. We'll tackle how to pitch effectively, what investors look for, and how to maintain control while bringing others on board. Let's get you funded and set for growth, because, without capital to fuel your dreams, even the best ideas can fizzle out.

Bootstrapping

Bootstrapping is the art of growing your business using limited resources, specifically your own funds or revenue generated from early sales. It's a process that requires a lot of grit and ingenuity, but for many entrepreneurs, it's the only viable option. The beauty of bootstrapping is that it forces you to be frugal and creative, ensuring that your business model is lean right from the start. You avoid incurring debt or giving away equity and build your company on a solid financial foundation you control.

One of the first steps in bootstrapping is cutting unnecessary costs and focusing solely on what's essential for your business to survive and grow. This means saying no to fancy offices, high-end software, and other luxuries that don't directly contribute to your bottom line. Instead, work from home or a co-working space, use free or affordable tools, and be cautious with every dollar you spend. The goal is to stretch your budget as much as possible while still delivering value to your customers.

Start by making a detailed budget, accounting for all expenses, even the smallest ones. Track your spending meticulously and always look for cheaper alternatives that don't compromise the quality of your product or service. Negotiation is your best friend here – don't hesitate to haggle prices with suppliers or negotiate better deals with service providers. Every penny saved is a penny that can be reinvested into your business.

A common misconception about bootstrapping is that it limits growth, but this isn't always the case. In fact, many successful companies started this way, growing methodically and sustainably. When you're bootstrapping, you're forced to test your ideas quickly and pivot when necessary. This ensures that your product or service meets market demand right from the outset, and if it doesn't, you'll know early enough to make necessary adjustments without having sunk enormous amounts of capital.

Generating initial revenue can be daunting, but it's crucial for survival. Focus on direct sales and getting those first paying customers. At this stage, your goal is to validate your business model. The feedback from your initial customers is invaluable, and generating revenue early can help reinvest into the business. Word of mouth can be a powerful tool. Treat your customers exceptionally well and incentivize them to spread the word. Your best marketing might come from those who buy from you first.

Bootstrapping also teaches resilience and resourcefulness. With limited funds, you'll need to wear multiple hats – from marketing and customer service to shipping and accounting. It's a hands-on experience that gives you an intimate understanding of your business's inner workings. This knowledge becomes invaluable as you grow, enabling you to identify inefficiencies and understand what's needed to scale effectively.

Another potent strategy in bootstrapping is building strategic partnerships. These partnerships can help you access resources and networks that would otherwise be beyond your reach. Find businesses that complement your own and offer mutually beneficial relationships. For example, if you run a small tech startup, partnering with a cybersecurity firm can enhance your services while expanding their market reach. Look for ways to cross-promote, bundle offers, or co-host events. These collaborations can significantly amplify your reach and credibility without further burdening your budget.

When it comes to hiring, think lean. Avoid the temptation to bring on full-time staff too early. Instead, consider freelancers or part-time workers to handle tasks that are outside your expertise or that you simply don't have time to manage. Platforms like Upwork or Fiverr offer access to a global talent pool at competitive rates. This way, you can get high-quality work done without the long-term commitment and overhead of full-time salaries.

Bootstrap-focused marketing is another critical area. Digital marketing offers substantial reach at a low cost if done right. Utilize social media channels, create engaging content, and leverage SEO to drive organic traffic to your website. Email marketing can particularly be effective for nurturing relationships with potential customers. The key here is consistency; regular updates and engagement keep your brand top of mind without requiring a hefty marketing budget.

Bootstrapping also means being a bit of a jack-of-all-trades. You'll need to become proficient in various areas from accounting to marketing to customer service. While this might sound overwhelming, it's an incredible learning experience that builds your skills and makes you a more versatile entrepreneur. It's also an opportunity to leverage low-cost educational resources. Utilize free online courses, webinars, and community meetups to build your knowledge and network.

Using the revenue generated to reinvest is another critical aspect of bootstrapping. Rather than paying yourself a large salary, consider living frugally and putting profits back into the business. This can fund further product development, marketing efforts, or even the occasional luxury that can give your business a professional edge. By continually reinvesting, you're sowing the seeds for future growth.

Bootstrap financing also gives you significant control over your business. Without outside investors, you retain full ownership, ensuring that all decisions align with your vision and goals. This autonomy can be liberating and empowering, allowing you to steer your company in the direction you believe is best without external pressures.

A good thing to consider is joining startup incubators or accelerators even when you're bootstrapping. These programs often provide mentorship, resources, and sometimes even capital in exchange for equity or other commitments. More importantly, they offer a network of like-minded entrepreneurs and seasoned professionals who can provide invaluable advice and support. While incubators do typically take equity, you'll need to weigh the benefits of these resources against the cost of giving up some control.

In addition, always have an emergency fund. The startup journey is filled with uncertainties, and having a financial cushion can mean the difference between survival and shutdown during rough patches. Aim to keep enough reserves to cover essential expenses for at least three to six months. This buffer can provide a vital safety net, allowing you to navigate through crises without panic.

Networking is another crucial component of successful bootstrapping. Attend industry conferences, join online communities, and never underestimate the power of a well-crafted LinkedIn profile. Networking isn't just about finding customers or partners; it's about learning from others, finding mentors, and sometimes stumbling upon opportunities you never knew existed. Always keep an ear to the ground for industry trends and shifts. Staying informed can help you anticipate changes and adapt quickly, keeping your bootstrapping journey agile and responsive.

To conclude, bootstrapping is a robust pathway for those willing to dig deep and harness every bit of creativity and resilience they have. It requires a balance of frugality, strategic planning, and relentless hustle. The skills and lessons you gain from bootstrapping are invaluable and often set the foundation for long-term business success. This journey isn't just about surviving; it's about thriving through innovative thinking and smart resource management. Get comfortable with being uncomfortable, and remember, every giant enterprise once started small.

Attracting Investors

Securing funding is often the most challenging part of starting and growing a business. When it comes to attracting investors, it's not just about having a great idea—it's about selling your vision, demonstrating your potential for growth, and proving that you've got the chops to make your business a roaring success. The act of drawing in investors is as much an art as it is a science, combining compelling storytelling, robust financial planning, and a clear path to profitability.

First things first, you need to understand what investors are looking for. The primary goal of any investor is to see a return on their investment. This means they need to believe that your business will not only succeed but will also thrive in a way that brings them significant returns. A well-crafted pitch deck highlighting key points such as market opportunity, competitive analysis, business model, and financial projections is essential. It's your roadmap to capturing investor interest.

Equally important is your ability to communicate your vision clearly and effectively. Investors are more inclined to back entrepreneurs who exhibit passion and confidence without sounding overly rehearsed. They want to see that you not only understand your market but also have a deep personal investment in solving a real problem. Your enthusiasm should be infectious, instilling them with a sense of urgency to get involved.

Financials make or break deals. Be prepared to dive deep into your numbers, showcasing detailed financial projections and break-even analyses. Transparency is crucial here. Investors need to see that you've thought through every scenario and have plans in place for potential risks. Financial acumen reassures investors that their money will be used wisely, increasing the chances of your business's success.

Networking can dramatically help in attracting investors. Attend industry meetups, pitch competitions, and entrepreneurial events to connect with potential investors. Recommendations and introductions from people within the industry can open doors that might otherwise remain closed. Personal relationships often tip the scales when an investor is deciding between two equally promising ventures.

Also, consider the type of investors you are targeting. Angel investors, venture capitalists, family offices, and crowdfunding platforms each have different criteria and benefits. Tailor your pitch to resonate with the specific interests and expectations of your targeted investor group. Angel investors might value personal chemistry more, while venture capitalists could be more numbers-driven. Crowdfunding, on the other hand, often hinges on the consumer appeal of your product or service.

Timing also plays a crucial role in the process. You should approach investors when you have reached significant milestones that demonstrate progress and potential. Whether it's completing a prototype, securing initial customers, or hitting specific revenue targets, these milestones reduce perceived risk and showcase momentum.

To attract investors, your business model should be scalable. Investors are looking for opportunities where they can see not just returns, but exponential growth. Your ability to articulate a scalable business model that covers market expansion, product diversification, or geographical outreach can be a huge selling point.

Next, let's talk about storytelling. Yes, that's right, storytelling. Investors get tons of pitches—what sets yours apart is a compelling narrative that interweaves your business's mission, vision, and potential impact. Humanize your data with stories about your customers, your inspirations, and your journey. A well-told story can make your pitch irresistible.

Pitching to potential investors is like an audition. Practice is key. Rehearse your pitch with mentors, advisors, or even friends to refine your delivery and anticipate questions. Constructive feedback can drastically improve your pitch. Make sure to polish not just your pitch deck but also your presentation skills. Confidence and clarity in your delivery are just as important as the content itself.

It's also wise to consider the idea of strategic partnerships. Many investors can provide more than just funding. Look for those who bring additional value — be it industry expertise, business connections, or operational support. These strategic partners can play a vital role in your business's success, offering mentoring and guidance beyond mere financial input.

Don't underestimate social proof. When credible people within your industry endorse your startup, it dramatically increases your credibility. Testimonials, advisory board members, or notable early adopters can serve as powerful endorsements that sway investor opinion in your favor.

One effective strategy is to create a fear of missing out (FOMO). Investors are more likely to jump on board if they believe others are also willing to back your venture. Subtly highlighting interest from other investors or emphasizing limited-time opportunities can create a sense of urgency.

Legal formalities and due diligence are inevitable steps in the investment process. Maintain proper documentation of your business activities, intellectual property, and financial statements. Investors often conduct thorough due diligence before committing, and any red flags in this process can jeopardize potential deals.

Finally, patience is vital. Attracting investors doesn't happen overnight. Be ready for multiple rounds of pitches, negotiations, and iterations on your business plan. Each interaction with a potential investor is a learning experience that brings you one step closer to successfully securing funding.

To sum it up, attracting investors requires a blend of strategic planning, effective communication, and relentless persistence. By understanding what investors want, delivering your vision compellingly, and backing it up with solid financials and proof of concept, you will increase your chances of successfully securing the investment needed to turn your entrepreneurial dreams into reality. Stay focused, stay passionate, and most importantly, stay resilient.

Chapter 4: The Grind (Months 0-4)

The first few months are going to be demanding, but they're also an exciting opportunity to lay the groundwork for lasting success. Through consistent effort and determination, you'll learn to navigate the complexities of finding your target customers, and molding an offer they can't resist. It's a period of trial and error, and yes, there will be late nights and early mornings. But every bit of hustle during this phase—a mix of research, networking, and raw perseverance—sets you up for future wins. Focus on getting your product into the hands of those who will become your biggest advocates, and remember, perfection is less important than progress. Momentum here isn't just an option; it's a necessity. Embrace the grind because the habits and systems you build now are the bedrock of your million-dollar journey.

Finding Your Target Customers

Alright, now that you've got your feet wet, it's time to dive into one of the most crucial parts of your journey: finding your target customers. You can have the best product in the world, but if you're not getting it in front of the right people, it's all for nothing. So, let's talk strategy.

First things first, who are these people? Your target customers are the individuals who are most likely to benefit from and be interested in your product. They're the ones who will drive your sales and, ultimately, your success. Identifying and understanding them will shape your marketing, product development, and overall business strategy. But finding them isn't a one-size-fits-all process. It's an ongoing effort that involves research, experimentation, and adaptability.

Start by creating a customer persona. This is a fictional character that represents your ideal customer and includes details like age, gender, income level, interests, and pain points. Dig deep and be specific. A mom in her 30s who works part-time and values convenience is a more useful persona than just "women aged 25-40." The more detailed your persona, the better you'll be at targeting and serving your customers.

Next, use data to validate your assumptions. Look at analytics on your social media platforms, websites, and any other digital touchpoints where you engage with your potential customers. Tools like Google Analytics can provide insights into who is visiting your site, what they're interested in, and how they interact with your content. Use this data to refine your customer persona and adjust your marketing strategies accordingly.

But data alone isn't enough. Get out there and talk to people. Yes, actually talk to them. The best insights often come from direct conversations with your potential customers. Set up surveys, conduct interviews, and organize focus groups. Ask them about their needs, preferences, and how they currently solve the problems your product addresses. This qualitative data will provide a richer understanding of your target audience than numbers ever could.

Social media is another goldmine for finding your target customers. Don't just post content and hope for the best. Engage in discussions relevant to your niche. Join groups, follow hashtags, and see what people are talking about. Pay attention to the language they use and the problems they discuss. This can give you clues about how to position your product and what features to highlight.

Also, consider your competitors. Who are they targeting? Study their marketing strategies, the language they use, and where they advertise. Sign up for their newsletters, follow their social media accounts, and see how they interact with their audience. While you should never copy them, understanding their tactics can help you identify gaps in the market that you can exploit.

It's essential to remember that finding your target customers isn't about excluding people. Rather, it's about focusing your efforts where they'll be most effective. A broad approach might seem like it casts a wider net, but it's often less effective than a targeted one. When you try to appeal to everyone, you often end up resonating with no one.

Now, let's talk about experimenting. Depending on your budget and resources, you can run different types of campaigns to see what works best. A/B testing is a great way to compare different versions of your ads, landing pages, or emails to see which performs better. These experiments don't have to be complex. Even small tweaks can lead to significant insights.

Email marketing can also be instrumental in targeting your audience effectively. Segment your email list based on customer personas, purchase history, and engagement levels. By sending tailored messages to different segments, you'll increase your chances of conversion and build stronger relationships with your customers.

Customer feedback is another vital tool. After launching your product, gather feedback aggressively. Use surveys, ask for reviews, and monitor social media chatter around your product. This information is invaluable for refining both your product and your understanding of your target audience. Remember, the goal isn't just to find customers, but to create loyal advocates for your brand.

Finally, stay nimble. The market is always evolving, and so are customer needs and behavior. Regularly revisit and update your customer personas based on new data and feedback. What worked last quarter might not work now. Stay informed about industry trends and continually test new approaches.

Finding your target customers is a process that requires curiosity, persistence, and adaptability. But get it right, and you'll set a solid foundation for achieving your $1 million goal. Remember, it's all about being customer-centric, listening to their needs, and finding innovative ways to meet them.

Now that you've got a clearer idea of who you're targeting, it's time to think about how to appeal to them. Up next, we'll dive into crafting an irresistible offer that they simply can't refuse. Stay focused, stay motivated, and let's keep grinding!

Crafting an Irresistible Offer

Picture this: you're in the early months of building your dream business, a period we've fondly dubbed "The Grind." These initial months (0-4) are when the rubber meets the road. You're not just finding your target customers; you're also crafting an offer that's so irresistible, they can't help but take action. This isn't a task you can afford to get wrong. After all, what's a groundbreaking product without an equally groundbreaking offer? So, how do you make your offer compelling enough to stand out in a crowded marketplace?

First, let's get one thing straight: an irresistible offer isn't just about what you're selling; it's about the value you're providing. You want your potential customers to see your offer and think, "I'd be crazy not to buy this!" Think about your offer as a package deal: it's not just the product but also the extras that make it special. These extras could be a guarantee, a bonus, a discount, or even a behind-the-scenes look at how your product works. The key here is to add elements that elevate the perceived value of your offer far beyond its actual cost.

Okay, let's break down the anatomy of an irresistible offer. At its core, your offer should have a clear, compelling promise. What immediate, tangible benefit will your customers get from your product? Will it save them time? Will it make them money? Will it improve their quality of life? The promise needs to resonate with the primary pain points or desires of your target audience. It's about solving a problem or fulfilling a need in a way that's straightforward yet profound.

Next, consider the risk reversal. One major reason people hesitate to make a purchase is the fear of making a bad decision. By incorporating a robust guarantee—say, a 30-day money-back guarantee—you remove this risk. This assurance can significantly lower the perceived risk, making the offer more appealing. When people feel there's no risk, they're more likely to take the plunge.

Bonuses are another powerful component. Think about additional features or services that complement your main product. These bonuses should be of

CHAPTER 4: THE GRIND (MONTHS 0-4)

high perceived value and relevance to your customer. For instance, if you're selling a fitness program, a bonus might be a free e-book on nutrition or a set of workout videos. The idea is to create an offer stack where each component adds more and more value, making the overall offer nearly impossible to refuse.

Now, let's dive into urgency and scarcity, two psychological triggers that can push potential customers over the edge to buy. Urgency can be created through limited-time offers or expiring discounts. Scarcity involves limiting the number of products available or offering exclusive deals. People are wired to avoid missing out, and these triggers can make your offer much more enticing. But be genuine—false scarcity can backfire and erode trust.

Language matters. The words you choose to describe your offer can make a world of difference. Use persuasive language that highlights benefits rather than features. Benefits resonate on an emotional level, while features speak logically. For example, instead of saying, "Our software has a user-friendly interface," you could say, "Easily save time and get more done with our intuitive software." The slight tweak in wording changes the impact significantly.

Another essential aspect is social proof. Showcasing testimonials, reviews, or case studies can build credibility and trust. People are more likely to buy something if they see others have had a positive experience with it. For a new venture, initial testimonials may come from beta testers or early adopters. These early endorsements can be incredibly persuasive and can significantly boost the attractiveness of your offer.

Pricing is the next crucial element. Your pricing strategy should reflect the value you're providing but also take into account your target market's willingness to pay. Consider offering multiple pricing tiers to cater to different segments. For instance, a basic, standard, and premium package could capture a wider audience. Each tier should have clear differentiators that justify the price increases. And don't forget—your pricing should also incorporate any bonuses or guarantees to highlight how much more customers are getting for their money.

Personalization isn't just a buzzword; it's a necessity. Tailoring your offer to specific customer segments can amplify its effectiveness. This means going beyond demographics and diving into psychographics—understanding their interests, values, and lifestyle choices. For example, if you know your target audience values sustainability, incorporating eco-friendly products or practices into your offer can make it more appealing.

Alright, here's an actionable framework: The Three Ps—Promise, Proof, and Price. Craft a compelling promise that speaks directly to your audience's primary concern. Back it up with credible proof, whether it's testimonials, case studies, or guarantees. Finally, present a price that reflects the immense value you're offering. Keep iterating this framework to find the right mix that resonates with your customers.

Don't underestimate the power of a well-crafted story. People connect with stories far more than they do with cold, hard facts. Share the journey of how your product came to be, the challenges you faced, and the passion that drives you. This narrative makes your offer more relatable and memorable. A good story can transform your offer from a mere transaction to an emotional experience.

Consider the user experience as part of your offer. A seamless, hassle-free buying process can be a significant part of making your offer irresistible. Make sure the checkout process is simple, clear, and quick. Implementing features like one-click purchase options, multiple payment methods, and instant confirmations can drastically improve the overall customer experience.

It's also worth mentioning the importance of follow-up. Once someone shows interest in your offer but doesn't immediately buy, don't let them slip through the cracks. Use follow-up emails, retargeting ads, or SMS reminders to keep your offer top-of-mind. Sometimes a gentle nudge is all it takes to convert interest into a sale.

Lastly, adapt and optimize. An irresistible offer isn't static; it's dynamic and evolves based on feedback and data. Run A/B tests to see what elements of your offer resonate most with your audience. Analyze conversion rates, customer feedback, and sales data to continuously refine and improve. The market is always changing, and your offer should be flexible enough to adapt to new trends and insights.

Crafting an irresistible offer is both an art and science. It requires a deep understanding of your audience, a commitment to providing exceptional value, and the agility to adapt and optimize. As you move through the first few months of your entrepreneurial journey, put these principles into practice. Your irresistible offer will serve as the cornerstone of your business success, paving the way to your first $1 million.

Launching Your Product

So, you've identified your target customers and crafted an irresistible offer. Now comes the pivotal point in the journey—launching your product. This is where all that hard work starts to pay off, but it can also be where things go sideways if you're not careful. Let's dive into what it takes to launch your product successfully and hit the ground running in these first four months.

Launching a product isn't just about flipping a switch. It's a calculated process that involves a lot of preparation, testing, and finally executing. One of the key components is building anticipation. You want people to be excited about your product before it's even available. Think of the buzz around a new iPhone release—Apple's mastered the art of creating a frenzy months ahead of the actual launch day.

To start with, consider a soft launch. This phase involves releasing your product to a select group of people like loyal customers or friends and family. A soft launch allows you to gather valuable feedback and make necessary adjustments without the risk of a full-scale public failure. It's your chance to work out the kinks and ensure everything is as close to perfect as it can be.

Social proof is your best friend during this period. Encourage those initial users to share their experiences and testimonials. Positive reviews from early adopters can go a long way in convincing others to take the plunge. Utilize social media platforms, online forums, and even email newsletters to amplify their voices. These testimonials act as free advertising and build credibility for your product.

Timing is everything. You don't want to launch during a period when people are less likely to make purchases. Seasonal products should be launched at the beginning of their respective seasons. If your product is universal, consider avoiding major holidays and peak vacation times unless those are precisely when your audience is most active.

Marketing efforts need to be omnipresent and cohesive. Leverage various channels like social media, email marketing, and even traditional advertising if it fits your target demographic. Each channel should reinforce your main message and create a unified brand experience. Consistency is crucial. You can't have your social media saying one thing and your emails something completely different.

Paid advertising can be a crucial element in scaling your reach quickly. Platforms like Facebook, Instagram, and Google Ads offer targeted advertising options that allow you to zero in on your exact demographics. However, don't blow your budget on ads right out the gate; start small, measure ROI, and scale up from there. Insights and analytics from these campaigns can help you fine-tune your messaging and target audience.

Having a compelling launch offer can also tilt the scales in your favor. Whether it's a discount, a buy-one-get-one-free deal, or some exclusive bonus, a compelling offer can provide that extra nudge to potential buyers who are on the fence. Just make sure that whatever offer you choose aligns with your long-term business goals and doesn't devalue your product.

Creating a sense of urgency can work wonders. Limited-time offers or limited stock warnings can push potential customers to act quickly. This strategy can drastically improve your conversion rates right from the start. Incorporate countdown timers on your website and in your marketing materials to visually reinforce this urgency.

Your website is your digital storefront—make sure it's ready for the rush. Double-check that all links work, the checkout process is smooth, and the page load times are minimal. A user-friendly website can significantly reduce cart abandonment rates and improve the overall customer experience. If you're not tech-savvy, hiring a professional to handle this could be a wise investment.

Pre-launch content can include blogs, vlogs, and how-to guides about your product or associated industry topics. This not only establishes you as an authority in your field but also drives organic traffic to your site. SEO strategies should be employed from the get-go to ensure your content ranks high on search engines. High-quality, keyword-rich content can truly set you apart.

It's crucial to have a robust customer service system in place. You shouldn't underestimate the power of good customer service, especially during a product launch. Make sure there are multiple channels for customer support, including live chat, email, and phone support. Quick responses and effective solutions will boost customer satisfaction and help mitigate any negative experiences.

A/B testing is another valuable tactic. Whether it's different ad copies, email headlines, or landing page designs, A/B testing allows you to see what resonates most with your audience. This data-driven approach takes a lot of guesswork out of the equation and can result in significantly higher conversion rates.

Finally, remember that launching your product is just the beginning. The real work starts as you continue to optimize, listen to feedback, and iterate based on what you learn. Keep an open line of communication with your customers—they're the best source of insights for future improvements.

Launching your product is an exhilarating experience that comes with its set of challenges. By preparing meticulously, utilizing strategic marketing, and listening to your audience, you can turn this initial phase into a catapult for your business. The grind is real, but the rewards can be monumental if executed well.

Chapter 5: First Sales Tactics

Alright, it's time to dive into the heart of any business: making that first sale. Your initial sales tactics should focus on creating urgency and leveraging early adopters to build momentum. Start by highlighting the scarcity of your product - limited quantities, special launch pricing, or time-sensitive offers can work wonders. Let your early buyers feel like insiders. Share your vision with them and make them a part of your journey, offering exclusive benefits for feedback and testimonials. This won't just build immediate revenue; it'll create raving fans who help spread the word. Remember, authenticity and value are your best sales tools at this stage. Innovate fearlessly, adapt quickly, and keep the customer's needs front and center.

Creating Urgency and Scarcity

Alright, you've got your product, and it's ready to hit the market. Now comes a crucial step: creating urgency and scarcity. Imagine a limited-time offer that makes your customers feel like they're missing out if they don't act now. This tactic isn't just about driving sales; it's about crafting a narrative that positions your product as a must-have.

First, let's talk about urgency. Urgency can manifest in many forms, but the most common way is through time-sensitive offers. People hate missing out. They hate the idea that they will lose an opportunity if they don't act fast. Limited-time discounts, flash sales, and "only available for the next 24 hours" promotions are effective ways to inject urgency into the buying process. Your customers need to feel that if they hesitate, they'll miss the boat.

One technique is a countdown timer on your product page. A simple countdown ticking away builds a subconscious pressure on your potential buyers. It shows them clearly that the offer has an expiration date, and they need to act before the time runs out. This isn't just a psychological trick—it's a genuine incentive for those who are on the fence to make a decision quickly.

But urgency doesn't have to be high-pressure all the time. It can also be achieved more subtly through messaging. Words and phrases like "Act now," "Limited time only," and "Don't miss out" are persuasive without feeling pushy. The goal is to strike a balance—enough pressure to entice but not overwhelm.

Now, let's dive into scarcity. This might be one of the oldest tricks in the book, but it holds relevance today. Scarcity makes people perceive something as more valuable. Think about it: you're more likely to buy something if you believe it's scarce. Items that are in short supply often feel more desirable, and this sentiment is what you aim to replicate.

Ever see those "Only 2 left in stock" notices on e-commerce sites? That's scarcity at work. By indicating that there are limited quantities available, you create a rush to purchase. Customers don't want to regret their indecision later. They need to feel that your product is special and won't be around forever.

Another practical application of scarcity is offering limited edition versions of your product. This creates a sense of exclusivity. People love owning something unique. It taps into their desire to be different and own something that not everyone can get their hands on. Even if the base product is the same, a limited-edition variant can ignite a buying frenzy.

However, you need to be careful with how you present scarcity. It has to be genuine. Consumers are smart, and they can spot fake scarcity from a mile away. If you're always running 'limited time' offers or showing 'low stock' notices that don't change, you risk losing trust. Authenticity is key here. When you say something is limited, it should genuinely be limited.

One more impactful way to create urgency and scarcity is by combining them. For example, release a limited number of products with a time-bound offer. This tactic doubles the impact— not only do customers think the item might run out, but they also have a very short window to make that decision.

Subscription services master this technique. Even big names like Amazon Prime Day and Black Friday employ this method effectively. They offer amazing deals, but only for a day or sometimes even just a few hours. This has people waiting at their keyboards, ready to purchase the moment the sale goes live. You want to create a similar buzz for your product.

Urgency and scarcity are not only about pricing and stock levels; they can also be linked to events. For instance, if you're running a webinar or a live event, having a limited number of seats can create a rush. The idea is the same: people want to be part of something exclusive and don't want to miss out on an 'only chance' opportunity.

Social proof can also complement urgency and scarcity. When potential customers see that others are buying quickly, it builds a sense of urgency for them to act as well. Think about those rolling carts that show "John from New York just bought this" on e-commerce sites. It's a small nudge, making others feel they should join in before it's too late.

Now, let's consider pre-launch tactics. Creating excitement and urgency before you even launch your product can be a game-changer. Setting up a waitlist or opening a pre-order can stoke the fire of anticipation. Tell your audience that only the first 100 people will get a special bonus or a lower price. This exclusivity will drive more people to commit early, boosting your initial momentum.

FOMO, or Fear of Missing Out, is a powerful psychological trigger you should leverage. Use it to your advantage by making people feel like acting now is in their best interest. Remember, the fear of loss is far more potent than the hope of gain. Make your audience believe they will miss out on something great if they don't act now.

Consider loyalty and reward programs tailored around urgency and scarcity. Offer time-limited bonus points, exclusive early access, or limited-time VIP offers. This doesn't only promote immediate sales, but it fosters customer loyalty and repeat purchases. It gives your customers a reason to keep coming back, knowing there will be new opportunities that are just as exclusive and urgent.

Creating urgency and scarcity isn't about manipulating your customers. It's about helping them make quick, confident decisions. It's a way to push them past the paralysis of choice, where too many options and too much time can lead to inaction. By strategically implementing these tactics, you're facilitating a smoother, faster customer journey—from curiosity to purchase.

Lastly, always analyze and iterate. Monitor the effectiveness of your urgency and scarcity campaigns. Use A/B testing to see what works best. Is it the countdown timer or the limited stock notification? Or perhaps the combination of both? Data will guide you to refine and perfect these tactics over time, ensuring that your approach remains fresh and effective.

Your journey to that first $1 million is as much about strategy as it is about perseverance. Employing urgency and scarcity in a thoughtful, genuine way can drive more significant results than you'd imagine. Keep these techniques in your toolkit as you navigate the exciting terrain of early sales, and watch how they transform tentative interest into solid, confident purchases.

Leveraging Early Adopters

Leveraging early adopters is one of the most potent strategies for achieving your first million in revenue. These enthusiasts are your golden ticket. They're the folks who jump at the chance to try new products and aren't afraid of a few flaws. They're driven by curiosity and the excitement of being ahead of the curve. This group of trailblazers can propel your product into the mainstream faster than any amount of traditional advertising.

First and foremost, understanding who these early adopters are and where to find them is crucial. Typically, they're tech-savvy individuals who hang out in niche communities—whether it's online forums, specific social media groups, or certain industry events. These places are fertile ground for planting the seeds of your brand. Don't underestimate the power of a well-placed post on a trending subreddit or an engaging tweet that catches the eye of influential micro-influencers.

So, how do you engage these early adopters effectively? Start by speaking their language. Authenticity is key. Early adopters can sniff out insincerity a mile away. They want to see the genuine passion that you have for your product. Share the story of your journey, detailing your triumphs and struggles. By showing them the real you, you tap into their innate desire to support visionary projects and innovative thinkers.

Consider offering exclusive incentives that make early adopters feel like they're part of an elite club. Limited-time discounts, early access to new features, or even branded merchandise can go a long way. This not only entices them to make a purchase but also encourages them to spread the word. Personalize these offerings whenever possible; personalized emails and thank-you notes can create a lasting impression.

Beta testing is another great tactic. Invite early adopters to be part of your beta phase, ensuring they feel esteemed and valued. This phase provides crucial feedback while cementing a relationship with your brand. Turn them into brand advocates by actively listening to their suggestions and making visible improvements based on their input. These interactions make them feel heard and valued, fostering loyalty and generating positive word-of-mouth.

Creating a strong community around your product is essential. Whether it's through a Facebook group, a Discord server, or a dedicated forum, provide a space for early adopters to come together. This not only allows them to share their experiences and tips but also strengthens their connection to your brand. Foster engagement through regular updates, exclusive content, and interactive events like Q&A sessions or live demonstrations.

It's imperative to maintain a two-way conversation with your early adopters. Keep them updated on your progress, challenges, and upcoming features. Transparency builds trust. Use surveys and feedback forms to understand their experience, and don't shy away from addressing any issues they bring up. Converting these insights into actionable steps shows that you prioritize their input, making them more likely to stay loyal.

Successful early adopter engagement often translates into organic growth. Their enthusiasm is infectious, and their recommendations carry weight. Encourage them to share their experiences on social media. User-generated content can be a game-changer. Reposting their reviews, testimonials, and unboxing videos can provide authentic and relatable content that resonates with potential customers.

In summary, leveraging early adopters is about more than just initial sales; it's about building a foundation of loyal, enthusiastic customers who can propel your business forward. By understanding their mindset and motivations, engaging them authentically, offering personalized incentives, and building a strong community, you create an army of advocates who are invested in your success. These early adopters will not only drive your initial sales but also lay the groundwork for your product's long-term success.

Chapter 6: Streamlining Operations

In the march toward that first million, refining how your business operates isn't just about cutting costs—though that's a bonus—it's about creating a well-oiled machine that runs smoothly without constant intervention. Imagine the day when your systems are so efficient, they almost manage themselves. You'll free up time to focus on strategy and growth, and that's where you truly start scaling. Introduce automation tools, optimize workflows, and ensure your inventory management is top-notch to avoid costly mistakes. By building efficient systems and fine-tuning inventory processes, you're not just saving time; you're making time for innovation and growth. Embrace the power of streamlined operations and watch your business transition from chaotic to controlled, setting the stage for the explosive growth chapters ahead.

Building Efficient Systems

When it comes to streamlining operations, the backbone of your success lies in building efficient systems. This isn't about creating a rigid structure that stifles creativity, but about implementing processes that save time, reduce errors, and ensure consistency. An efficient system is your silent partner, working tirelessly behind the scenes so you can focus on growing your business.

First and foremost, understand that efficiency isn't synonymous with cutting corners. It's about maximizing output with the minimum input without compromising on quality. The most successful entrepreneurs have

CHAPTER 6: STREAMLINING OPERATIONS

recognized this and invested time in crafting systems that automate repetitive tasks and streamline decision-making.

Start with identifying the core activities that drive your business. These could be anything from order processing to customer support. List them down and analyze which tasks take up most of your time or are prone to mistakes. This is where you can introduce automation tools to alleviate some of the burdens.

Automation doesn't mean replacing the human touch with robots; it means leveraging technology to handle routine tasks, thereby freeing up your team to engage in more strategic, high-value activities. It can be as simple as setting up automated email responses for customer inquiries or integrating a CRM system to manage customer relationships efficiently.

Speaking of customer relationship management (CRM), this is a cornerstone for building efficient systems. A robust CRM allows you to track interactions with customers, manage leads, and streamline communication. Systems like Salesforce or HubSpot can be game-changers when it comes to maintaining seamless operations. They not only centralize your customer data but also offer analytics that can guide your strategy.

No system can be efficient if your team isn't aligned. Constant communication and training are crucial to ensuring everyone knows how to use the tools at their disposal effectively. Hold regular training sessions to keep your team updated on any new systems or updates to existing ones. This keeps everyone on the same page and mitigates the risks associated with human error.

Another key to building efficient systems is to adopt a mindset of continuous improvement. Regularly review your processes to identify bottlenecks or areas of inefficiency. Encourage feedback from your team because they are often the ones who interact with these systems daily and can provide valuable insights. Implement the feedback to iterate and improve your systems.

Next, integrate your various systems to ensure they work seamlessly together. Data silos can be a major hurdle in achieving operational efficiency. Use APIs and other integration tools to make sure information flows freely between your CRM, inventory management, and accounting systems. This ensures that your data is always up-to-date, reducing errors and saving time spent on manual updates.

Now, let's talk about inventory management, a crucial aspect of building efficient systems, especially for product-based businesses. Poor inventory management can lead to stockouts or overstock, both of which are costly. Use inventory management software like Zoho Inventory or TradeGecko to keep track of stock levels in real-time. Automate reorder points so you're not caught off guard by low stock levels. Efficient inventory systems help maintain the delicate balance between supply and demand, ensuring you can meet customer needs without tying up too much capital in unsold goods.

Financial management is another area where efficient systems pay off. Tools like QuickBooks or Xero can automate many aspects of your bookkeeping, from invoicing to payroll, ensuring you have accurate, real-time financial data. This helps you make informed decisions quickly. An efficient financial system can also help you manage cash flow better, ensuring you have enough liquidity to invest in growth opportunities.

A word on scalability: as your business grows, so too will the complexity of your operations. An efficient system shouldn't just work for now; it should be scalable to handle increased loads. This is why investing in cloud-based solutions can be beneficial. Cloud systems offer flexibility and scalability, allowing you to add features and handle more data as your business expands.

Don't overlook the importance of cybersecurity in your efficient systems. Protecting your data is paramount. Implement strong cybersecurity measures like multi-factor authentication, encrypted databases, and regular security audits. An efficient system is not just about performance; it's also about ensuring your operations are secure and compliant with regulations.

Lastly, remember that building an efficient system isn't a one-time task. It's an ongoing process that requires regular monitoring and adjustments. Set aside time each quarter to review your systems, look at performance metrics, and make necessary tweaks. By doing this, you ensure that your operations remain lean, efficient, and capable of supporting your business objectives.

In summary, building efficient systems is about creating a robust infrastructure that supports your business goals. It involves strategic use of technology, continual team training, regular process reviews, and a commitment to agility and improvement. By focusing on these elements, you can free up valuable time, reduce costs, and build a solid foundation for scalable growth. The more efficient your systems, the more room you have to innovate and expand, bringing you closer to that first $1 million milestone.

Managing Inventory

Managing inventory can be one of the trickiest parts of running a business, especially when you're striving to scale operations and hit that $1 million mark. The key to success is creating a balance between meeting customer demand and minimizing overstock. Nobody wants to be stuck with piles of unsold products or, worse, face delays because of stock shortages. Both scenarios can hurt your bottom line.

First things first, let's talk about inventory management systems. Investing in a robust inventory management software can save you a lot of headaches. These systems help automate the tracking of stock levels, orders, sales, and deliveries. In the early stages, a simple spreadsheet might do the trick, but as your business grows, you'll need something more sophisticated. Consider systems that offer real-time analytics and integrate seamlessly with your e-commerce platform.

Understanding your turnover rates is crucial. High turnover rates generally indicate strong sales, but they can also mean you're operating with lower inventory levels, which can be risky. Conversely, low turnover may indicate stagnant inventory, tying up your cash in unsold products. Analyzing these rates helps you pinpoint which products are moving fast and which ones are staying on the shelves longer than they should.

One technique you'll want to implement is Just-In-Time (JIT) inventory. This method involves ordering and receiving inventory only as it is needed in the production process, minimizing storage costs. The downside? It requires reliable suppliers and accurate demand forecasts. Any hiccups in the supply chain can lead to delays, so consider your relationship with suppliers and the reliability of your data before fully committing to JIT.

Another critical strategy is demand forecasting. Use historical sales data, market trends, and even seasonality to predict what your inventory needs will be. Machine learning algorithms can be particularly useful here, offering predictive analytics to help you make more informed decisions. The more data you can feed into these systems, the better they'll perform.

Don't forget about safety stock – the buffer that protects you against fluctuations in demand and supply chain disruptions. While too much safety stock can be a cash drain, too little can leave you vulnerable to stockouts. Finding that sweet spot is key, and sometimes it requires a bit of trial and error.

Seasonality plays a role in inventory management, too. If your business sells seasonal products, effective inventory planning becomes even more critical. Understanding the cyclical nature of your sales will help you optimize stock levels throughout the year. For example, if you're selling winter apparel, you'll need to ramp up inventory before the cold season hits and gradually taper it off as spring approaches.

Supplier relationships also play a massive role. Good relationships with your suppliers can lead to perks like favorable pricing, priority service, and even insights into market trends. Foster these relationships by maintaining open lines of communication. Regularly review their performance and have backup suppliers ready just in case something goes awry. It's all about being prepared for any scenario.

Investing in a warehouse management system (WMS) can further streamline your inventory processes. A WMS can help improve accuracy and efficiency by guiding inventory putaway, replenishment, and picking processes. This technology reduces human error and allows you to track every item in your warehouse, ensuring nothing gets lost or misplaced.

Implement barcode scanning or RFID (Radio-Frequency Identification) systems to improve accuracy in inventory tracking. Barcodes and RFID tags make it easier to track items throughout the supply chain, from receiving and storage to picking and shipping. These tag systems also help in conducting faster and more accurate stock counts.

Automation can't be ignored. From automated stock-taking to reordering alerts, automation can significantly cut down on manual labor and errors. Set up automated reorder points for your most crucial items. When stock levels hit a predefined threshold, the system can trigger a reorder, ensuring you're never caught off guard by low inventory levels.

Inventory audits should be part of your regular routine. These audits help you verify the accuracy of your inventory records and identify any discrepancies. Cycle counting, where you count a small subset of your inventory on a regular basis, allows for ongoing checks without massive disruptions. It's a lot less daunting than doing a full inventory check all at once, and it can pinpoint issues early.

Lastly, pay attention to your *dead stock*, the inventory that doesn't sell. Dead stock not only clutters your warehouse but also ties up capital that could be better used elsewhere. Conduct regular reviews to identify slow-moving items and use tactics like discounts or bundling to move these products out the door. Sometimes, cutting your losses and clearing out old stock is more beneficial than hanging onto it.

Remember, inventory management is not a set-it-and-forget-it task. It requires regular attention and refinement. Keep testing different strategies, analyzing your data, and adjusting your approach to find what works best for your business. Effective inventory management can reduce costs, improve cash flow, and significantly boost your profitability, bringing you one step closer to that $1 million goal.

Managing inventory may not always be glamorous, but it's a fundamental part of growing any successful business. By employing a combination of technology, strategic planning, and regular reviews, you can keep your operations lean and efficient. Take control of your inventory, and watch as it propels your business towards greater heights.

Chapter 7: The Growth (Months 5-8)

By the time you hit months five through eight, you're likely feeling the mounting excitement of tangible progress. This phase is all about amplifying your efforts and leveraging every win. Fine-tune your advertising strategy, making every dollar count, particularly if you're on a tight budget. Expand your marketing channels in ways that don't break the bank, but enhance your brand's visibility. This is the period where strategic scaling becomes crucial; the systems you've set up earlier need to operate like a well-oiled machine to support your growth spurt. Track your metrics closely and be ready to pivot when necessary. It's about building on your early successes and gearing up for the momentum that will take you into the next crucial stage of your journey.

Advertising on a Budget

Marketing is like the wind to your entrepreneurial sails, and in months 5-8, you'll need to harness it smartly, especially if you're counting pennies. Advertising on a budget doesn't mean skimping on effectiveness; it's about being resourceful, creative, and, above all, strategic. These months are crucial as you aim to transition from just surviving to thriving. But how do you make that leap without burning a hole in your pocket?

First, let's talk about the magic of social media—a haven for budget-conscious advertisers. Sites like Facebook, Instagram, Twitter, and LinkedIn offer powerful ad tools that allow hyper-targeting. With a little money, you can reach hundreds, if not thousands, of potential customers. The key is to start small, test your ads, and then scale up what works. One of the best-kept secrets is using custom audiences—target people based on their interests, behaviors, and even past interactions with your brand.

It's a good practice to collaborate with micro-influencers. Unlike mega-celebrities, micro-influencers have niche audiences that trust them. A shoutout or product review from them can drive significant traffic and sales. Often, these influencers don't charge exorbitant fees. Instead, they may accept free products or commissions on sales—keeping your costs low while leveraging their engagement.

Another effective tactic is tapping into the power of word-of-mouth marketing. Encourage your satisfied customers to share their experiences on social media. Create shareable content that makes it easy for them to spread the word. Social proof is compelling; people trust recommendations from friends and family more than any advertisement. You could even run referral programs offering discounts or freebies to customers who bring in new business.

Email marketing is another low-cost, high-impact strategy. Building an email list allows you to communicate directly with potential and existing customers. Your emails should provide value—think exclusive discounts, useful tips, and inside information about upcoming products or events. Email marketing tools like Mailchimp or ConvertKit offer free tiers for small businesses, making it easier to manage campaigns without spending much.

Don't overlook content marketing. Start a blog and focus on issues that resonate with your target audience. By providing valuable, free content, you'll attract organic traffic to your site. Over time, this helps establish your brand as an authority in your niche. Don't just stick to written content; diversify with videos, infographics, and podcasts. All these mediums can be produced at a relatively low cost but have a high potential for engagement.

While digital strategies are essential, traditional methods shouldn't be completely ignored. Print flyers, posters, and banners can be highly effective if placed in relevant, high-traffic areas. Local community boards, coffee shops, and even libraries offer spaces where your target audience might frequent. The cost for printing is minimal, especially if you start small and scale based on results. Sometimes, a well-placed flyer can bring in more customers than an expensive online ad.

Another local tactic is hosting events or workshops. It doesn't have to be anything grand; even a small gathering can create buzz. These events provide a platform to interact directly with potential customers, showcase your product, and receive instant feedback. Partnering with local businesses can further reduce costs and mutual benefits, such as splitting the expenses and tapping into each other's customer base.

Networking is an invaluable yet often overlooked method of marketing. Join local business associations, attend industry conferences, and make use of online communities like LinkedIn groups. These platforms can offer opportunities to share your brand story and reach new customers without the need for expensive advertising. Plus, the connections you make can lead to collaborations that benefit all parties involved.

Remember the power of retargeting. This marketing strategy involves re-engaging users who've previously visited your site but didn't make a purchase. Tools like Google AdWords and Facebook Pixel allow you to track these visitors and show them tailored ads. Because these potential customers are already familiar with your brand, they're more likely to convert, offering a higher ROI for your ad spend.

Utilizing SEO (Search Engine Optimization) is another low-cost strategy with long-term benefits. Optimizing your website content to rank higher in search engine results can drive organic traffic. Start with keyword research to identify the terms your potential customers are searching for. Integrate these keywords naturally into your content to improve your search engine rankings. Over time, better SEO will reduce the need for paid advertising.

Cross-promotional partnerships can also boost your advertising efforts on a budget. Find businesses that aren't direct competitors, but serve a similar audience. By promoting each other's products or services, both parties can expand their reach without incurring significant additional costs. Think of it as a win-win situation—a customer-base exchange program, if you will.

Utilize guerrilla marketing tactics. This involves unconventional, creative ways to market your product that cost very little. Street art, flash mobs, or even creative use of public spaces can generate buzz for your brand. These tactics can go viral online, reaching a much larger audience than initially anticipated. The key here is creativity and a deep understanding of your audience's interests and behaviors.

Always be aware of analytics and data. Measure the performance of every advertising tactic you deploy. Use free tools like Google Analytics to track where your website traffic comes from and how visitors interact with your site. By measuring your campaigns' effectiveness, you can make data-driven decisions to refine your strategies and ensure every dollar spent contributes to your growth.

The essence of advertising on a budget lies in leveraging the resources at your disposal in the most efficient way. Be resourceful, think outside the box, and always be willing to pivot based on what the data tells you. Budget constraints can be a blessing in disguise, pushing you to innovate, be more strategic, and ultimately, more successful. Whether through digital or traditional channels, the primary focus should be on understanding your target audience and delivering messages that resonate with them. That's how you'll not only survive but thrive in these critical growth months.

Scaling Your Marketing Efforts

It's game time for your business. You've got some sales under your belt, your operations are running smoothly, and now you're ready to scale up your marketing efforts. This phase is critical—you'll move from making sporadic sales to creating a consistent, booming revenue stream. This is where you transition from being a small player in the market to becoming a formidable force. Scaling your marketing efforts during months 5 to 8 is about widening your net, capturing more leads, and converting them into loyal customers.

First off, let's talk about leveraging data. At this stage, you should already have some customer data from your initial sales. Analyze this data to understand buyer patterns, preferences, and behaviors. Use tools like Google Analytics or customer relationship management (CRM) systems to gather insights. These insights will help you fine-tune your advertising strategies, allowing you to focus on channels and methods that yield the highest returns.

However, scaling isn't just about doing more of what works. It's also about experimenting with new strategies and channels. Diversify your marketing efforts by trying out different platforms. If you've been primarily using Facebook Ads, maybe it's time to explore LinkedIn or Instagram ads as well. Each platform has its own unique set of users, and tapping into multiple platforms can help you reach a broader audience.

Content is king, and it's even more vital when scaling up. By now, your content strategy should include a mix of blog posts, videos, social media posts, and possibly even podcasts. Aim to create valuable content that addresses the needs and interests of your target audience. Consistent, high-quality content can drive organic traffic to your site, improve your search engine ranking, and establish your authority in the industry.

Automation will be your best friend during this phase. Use marketing automation tools to handle repetitive tasks such as email marketing, social media posting, and lead nurturing. Tools like Mailchimp, HubSpot, or Hootsuite can help streamline these processes, freeing up your time to focus on strategy and creativity. Automated email campaigns, for instance, can keep your audience engaged without requiring constant manual effort.

You can't ignore the importance of SEO (Search Engine Optimization) when scaling. Investing time and resources into SEO can yield long-term benefits by driving organic traffic to your website. Make sure your website is optimized for relevant keywords, and consider creating blog content optimized for search engines. SEO isn't a quick win—it's a marathon. However, the effort you put in now will pay off in the long run by providing a steady stream of organic traffic.

Paid advertising will also play a substantial role in scaling your marketing efforts. As you increase your budget, refine your ad campaigns for better performance. Split testing—or A/B testing—your ads is essential. Test different headlines, images, call-to-actions, and even audience segments to see what works best. This iterative approach ensures that your ad spend is used most effectively, maximizing your return on investment (ROI).

Social proof becomes increasingly vital as you scale up. Testimonials, reviews, and case studies can significantly influence potential customers. Featuring positive reviews on your website and social media channels can build trust and credibility. If you've got satisfied customers, ask them for a testimonial or review. People are more likely to buy when they see others have had positive experiences with your product or service.

Think about partnerships. Collaborating with influencers or other brands can amplify your reach. Influencer marketing can be powerful; when an influencer endorses your product, it lends you credibility and exposes you to a larger, yet targeted, audience. Consider arranging for partnerships such as joint webinars, co-branded content, or product bundles. This kind of collaborative marketing can be a win-win situation for both parties involved.

Retargeting is another technique worth mentioning. Not everyone will convert the first time they visit your site. Retargeting campaigns help you recapture those leads who have shown interest but haven't yet made a purchase. Platforms like Facebook and Google offer robust retargeting options. Tailor your retargeting ads to remind visitors of what they're missing out on and entice them to come back.

Budget management becomes crucial during this time. It's easy to get carried away with spending in efforts to scale quickly. However, monitor your expenses and ROI meticulously. Allocate your budget towards channels that provide the best returns, but also set aside a portion for experimentation. Marketing, much like any other business activity, should be a balance of tried-and-true techniques and new ventures.

As your marketing efforts scale, so should your team. Depending on your budget and needs, you might consider hiring additional staff or contracting freelancers. Whether it's content creation, graphic design, or paid ad management, having specialized skills on your team can make a huge difference. Ensure everyone is aligned with your vision and goals, fostering a culture of collaboration and innovation.

Of course, scaling your marketing efforts doesn't mean you should forget your early supporters. Nurture relationships with your early adopters and loyal customers. They can become ambassadors for your brand, spreading the word about your products through word-of-mouth referrals. Customer-centric strategies, like loyalty programs and exclusive offers, can keep these valuable customers engaged.

Observe your competitors. Analyze what they're doing—both what works and what doesn't. Competitor analysis not only gives you ideas but also helps you avoid pitfalls they may have encountered. Tools like SEMrush or Ahrefs can provide insights into their SEO strategies, ad campaigns, and keywords.

Brand messaging consistency is another pivotal aspect. As you broaden your marketing efforts, maintaining a consistent brand voice is critical. Your branding should convey the same message, whether it's on your website, social media, or printed materials. This consistency helps in building and reinforcing brand recognition and trust.

Finally, never underestimate the power of feedback. Gather feedback from your marketing campaigns, customers, and even your team. Use this information for continuous improvement. Metrics and KPIs (Key Performance Indicators) should be your guiding star, helping you make data-driven decisions. Track conversions, customer acquisition costs, and lifetime value to fine-tune your strategies.

In essence, scaling your marketing is about smart growth. It's about leveraging data, diversifying your channels, creating compelling content, and maintaining consistency while experimenting with new ideas. It requires a balanced approach, combining creativity with analytical thinking. This journey from months 5 to 8 will lay the foundation for your business to thrive and soar, taking you one step closer to that elusive first $1 million.

Chapter 8: Achieving 25 Sales Per Day

Hitting the milestone of 25 sales per day isn't just a numbers game; it's about creating a well-oiled machine that converts interest into action consistently. Start by honing in on your conversion rates – small tweaks to your website's layout, copy, or checkout process can lead to significant gains. Utilize retargeting strategies to re-engage visitors who showed interest but didn't commit. Think of it as gently nudging them back to your offer with perfectly timed follow-ups. Equip yourself with data and adjust your tactics based on what's resonating with your audience. Remember, this is the stage where persistence and precision pay off – keep optimizing and retargeting until hitting 25 daily sales becomes your new normal.

Optimizing Conversion Rates

When it comes to achieving 25 sales per day, optimizing your conversion rates is critical. This isn't just about driving more traffic to your site; it's about making sure that the visitors you do attract are compelled to purchase. Improving your conversion rates—how many visitors turn into buyers—can have a tremendous impact on your daily sales numbers and, ultimately, your bottom line.

First off, let's clarify what we mean by "conversion rates." In simple terms, it's the percentage of visitors to your website who take a desired action, like making a purchase or signing up for a newsletter. Specifically, for achieving 25 sales per day, the focus is on purchase conversions. If you're currently converting 1% of your traffic and doubling that to 2%, you're looking at a significant increase in sales without needing additional traffic. It's a game of percentages, and a tight game at that.

One of the most effective ways to optimize conversion rates is through A/B testing. This involves creating two different versions of a webpage or ad and testing them against each other to see which performs better. The changes can be as subtle as tweaking a headline or as significant as redesigning a landing page. Tools like Google Optimize and Optimizely offer robust A/B testing features that can help you make data-driven decisions. The idea here is to keep testing in small increments, continually refining what works and discarding what doesn't.

Another crucial factor is your website's load time. Studies show that a 1-second delay in load time can lead to a 7% reduction in conversions. People have short attention spans; if your site takes too long to load, they'll bounce before even seeing what you have to offer. To address this, you should consider image compression, leveraging browser caching, and minimizing HTTP requests. Faster load times improve user experience, which directly correlates to higher conversion rates.

Your value proposition must be crystal clear within the first few seconds of a visitor landing on your site. You want to answer the question: "Why should I buy from you rather than anyone else?" This can be achieved through compelling copy, strong visuals, and clear calls-to-action. Each element on your site should guide users toward taking the action you desire—making a purchase. Every button, every piece of text, and every image should serve a function.

Understanding your customer's journey is another vital aspect. From the moment they land on your page to the final click of the purchase button, each step should be smooth and intuitive. This is where user experience (UX) design comes into play. Are your forms too long? Is your checkout process cumbersome? Each potential friction point can decrease your conversion rate. Therefore, simplifying the user journey increases the likelihood of conversions.

Social proof is powerful. Testimonials, reviews, and ratings can significantly affect purchasing decisions. Showcasing positive feedback and high ratings can build trust and credibility, which are crucial for converting visitors into buyers. People feel safer buying from a store that others trust. Don't just take my word for it; even a simple "Best Seller" tag can increase your conversion rate dramatically. Authenticity is key, so be honest with your reviews—fake or overly polished testimonials can do more harm than good.

Personalization can also play a role in optimizing conversion rates. Utilize data analytics to understand your customer demographics and buying behaviors. Tailor your marketing messages and website content to address their specific needs and interests. This could be as simple as suggesting products based on past purchases or as complex as personalized email campaigns. When customers feel understood, they're more likely to buy.

Next up is leveraging urgency and scarcity, which taps into human psychology. Limited-time offers or low-stock messages can create a sense of urgency, prompting visitors to make a purchase decision more quickly. However, use these tactics carefully. Overuse or exaggeration can lead to mistrust, which is counterproductive.

One often-overlooked aspect is mobile optimization. A significant portion of web traffic now comes from mobile devices. Ensure that your website is mobile-friendly, meaning it should look good and operate smoothly on any device. A responsive design is essential, as a poor mobile experience can severely limit your conversion rates.

Retargeting campaigns are also an effective strategy. On average, only 2% of visitors convert on their first visit to a website. Retargeting helps bring back the remaining 98% by showing them relevant ads as they browse other sites. Google Ads and Facebook Ads offer robust retargeting options to keep your brand in front of potential customers, increasing the likelihood they'll return and make a purchase.

Content plays a crucial role as well. High-quality, relevant content can educate, engage, and encourage visitors to become buyers. Use blogs, videos, and infographics to provide value and subtly steer prospects toward conversion. Great content builds trust and positions your brand as an authority in your niche, making people more likely to buy from you.

Finally, analytics are your best friend when it comes to optimizing conversion rates. Regularly review your metrics to see what's working and what's not. Google Analytics is a powerful tool that can provide insights into user behavior, traffic sources, and conversion funnels. Use this data to make informed decisions and continuously optimize your strategies.

In summary, achieving 25 sales per day isn't an overnight miracle but a systematic process. It involves understanding your audience, creating an optimal user experience, and leveraging data-driven strategies to continuously refine your approach. From A/B testing and load times to personalization and retargeting campaigns, each element plays a vital role in converting visitors into loyal customers. By focusing on these tactics, you'll not only improve your conversion rates but also move closer to hitting and surpassing your daily sales targets.

Remember, the road to your first $1 million is paved with lots of small but significant wins in optimizing your conversion rates.

Retargeting Strategies

Reaching your goal of 25 sales per day isn't just about getting new eyes on your product; it's also about making sure those who have already shown interest don't slip through the cracks. That's where retargeting strategies come in. Retargeting is your secret weapon, showcasing your product repeatedly to those who have already visited your site but didn't pull the trigger. It's not aggressive, it's strategic. Let's break this down.

First, you need to understand the power of cookies. No, not the delicious kind, but the small codes that track user behavior on your website. When someone visits your site and browses through your products, cookies allow you to follow up with ads that remind them of the items they looked at. Keep it casual; think of it like a gentle nudge rather than a hard sell.

Setting up retargeting pixels is simple but crucial. Whether you're using Google Ads, Facebook, or another platform, make sure you install these snippets of code on your site. These pixels will gather data on your visitors and enable you to retarget them with personalized ads across various platforms.

A key point to remember is segmentation. Not all visitors are the same, and neither should your ads be. Segment your audience based on their behavior. Did they just visit your homepage, or did they add items to their cart but abandon it at the last second? Each group requires a different message. For those who merely visited, a reminder of the benefits of your product could do the trick. For cart abandoners, you might want to sweeten the deal with a limited-time discount or free shipping offer.

Speaking of incentives, leverage them wisely. If someone has added items to their cart but hasn't checked out, offer a small discount or free shipping. This could be the final nudge they need. Too many businesses shy away from offering discounts, fearing it'll cut into profits, but think about it this way: a little discount can lead to a lot of sales, especially from customers who might not have purchased otherwise.

Visual appeal matters. Your retargeting ads need to be eye-catching and relevant. Use high-quality images of your products, and make sure your ad copy is concise yet compelling. A short testimonial or a punchy tagline can make all the difference. Don't make your ad too busy; simplicity often works best.

Dynamic retargeting can take things to the next level. Instead of showing generic ads, you can display ads featuring the exact products a visitor looked at. This level of personalization is highly effective because it feels like you're speaking directly to their interests, rather than a blanket ad meant for everyone.

Email retargeting is another potent tool. Capture email addresses wherever you can—whether through a signup form on your site or during the checkout process. Once you have these emails, follow up with a series of automated emails targeting different actions taken by the user. If someone abandoned their cart, send a friendly reminder. If someone browsed but didn't buy, inform them about a special promotion or new arrivals.

Let's talk about frequency. You don't want to bombard your potential customers to the point of annoyance, but you do want to stay top-of-mind. A balanced approach is key. Rotate your ads frequently and set frequency caps to ensure you're not overexposing your audience. Too many ads can lead to "ad fatigue," where people start ignoring your ads altogether.

Test, analyze, and adapt. What works for one audience might not work for another. Use A/B testing to see which versions of your ads perform best. Analytics will be your best friend here; scrutinize engagement rates, click-through rates, and conversion rates. This data will guide you in refining your retargeting strategies for optimal performance.

Mobile retargeting cannot be ignored. Most people are glued to their phones, and a good chunk of online purchases are made via mobile devices. Ensure your retargeting ads are optimized for mobile—fast loading, visually appealing, and easy to click through. This approach can significantly impact your conversion rates.

Consider timing. Catching your potential customers at the right moment is crucial. Retargeting ads should appear when they're most likely to act. Analyze your data to find out when your audience is most responsive, and strategically time your ads around these periods.

And let's not forget about social proof. People are influenced by what others are doing. Incorporate user-generated content or testimonials in your retargeting ads. When visitors see others enjoying your products, they're more likely to get on board. This kind of social validation can often tip the scales.

Don't underestimate the power of multi-channel retargeting. Don't just stick to one platform. Use a combination of Google, Facebook, Instagram, and even LinkedIn if it makes sense for your product. The more touchpoints you have, the better chances you have of converting those lukewarm leads into hot sales.

Let's be real: achieving 25 sales per day isn't going to happen overnight. But with effective retargeting strategies, you're putting yourself in a strong position to reach—and maybe even surpass—that goal. Use these strategies wisely and watch as those seemingly lost opportunities turn into loyal customers.

Chapter 9: Expanding Your Reach

Now that you've set the stage for steady sales, it's time to elevate your game by expanding your reach. Imagine tapping into networks that you've never accessed before, driving traffic and sales like never before. Collaborating with influencers allows you to leverage their established credibility and vast audiences, giving you instant visibility. On the other hand, a robust social media marketing strategy ensures you're engaging with potential customers regularly, keeping your brand top-of-mind. Balance creativity with analytics; test different campaigns, measure their impact, and double down on what works. This chapter is all about harnessing external forces to amplify your message, broadening your brand's footprint, and setting the stage for exponential growth. Gear up for innovative strategies that will catapult your business into new territories.

Influencer Partnerships

In today's digital age, influencer partnerships have emerged as a game-changing strategy for expanding your reach. This approach leverages the credibility and audience of social media personalities to spread the word about your product or service. But partnering with influencers is more than just a simple shout-out; it's about building mutual relationships that can drive substantial growth for your business.

To start, you'll need to identify influencers who resonate with your brand's values and target audience. Don't just go for the biggest names; sometimes, micro-influencers, with their smaller but highly engaged followers, can be more effective. Start by researching influencers in your niche, checking their engagement rates, and examining the quality of their content. Once you have a list, it's time to make your pitch.

Crafting a compelling pitch is crucial. Influencers get countless partnership requests daily, so you need to stand out. Personalize your message by mentioning specific posts of theirs you liked and explaining how your product aligns with their brand. Offering them something valuable in return, whether it's monetary compensation, free products, or affiliate commissions, is vital. Make it clear what's in it for them.

Once you've secured a partnership, the next step is to define the terms of collaboration. Lay out the objectives, deliverables, deadlines, and metrics for measuring success. Being clear about these aspects can prevent misunderstandings down the line. Offering creative freedom to the influencer ensures the promotion feels authentic, which is paramount for maintaining their audience's trust.

Authenticity is the cornerstone of any successful influencer partnership. Audiences are savvy; they can easily detect inauthentic endorsements. Encourage influencers to share genuine experiences with your product, even if it means highlighting a drawback. Transparency fosters trust and long-term loyalty from potential customers.

Monitoring the performance of an influencer campaign is essential for understanding its impact and refining your strategy. Utilize tracking links, unique discount codes, or even dedicated landing pages to gauge effectiveness. Metrics like engagement rates, click-through rates, and conversion rates will paint a clear picture of your campaign's success.

One success story to illustrate this point is a small skincare brand that collaborated with beauty influencers to review new product lines. By sending free samples and offering exclusive first-look content, the brand quickly generated buzz and saw a significant spike in sales. The influencers' genuine reviews and tutorials provided potential customers with the information and trust they needed to make a purchase.

Effective influencer partnerships aren't just about one-off collaborations. Building long-term relationships with influencers can amplify your reach even further. Regularly engaging with them, acknowledging their contributions, and maybe even involving them in product development can turn them into genuine advocates for your brand.

Cross-promotion is another tactic to maximize the reach of your influencer partnerships. Encourage influencers to share their content across multiple platforms, including blogs, YouTube, Instagram, and even TikTok. The more channels you utilize, the broader your reach becomes. This multi-channel approach helps ensure that your product stays top-of-mind and reaches various audience segments.

Speaking of different platforms, tailoring your campaign to suit the strengths of each is vital. A partnership on Instagram, for instance, might involve visually appealing photos and stories, whereas a YouTube collaboration could focus on in-depth product reviews or tutorials. Knowing the platforms well will allow you to craft campaigns that resonate more effectively with each audience.

Don't overlook the potential of user-generated content. Encouraging influencers to motivate their followers to create content related to your brand can expand your reach organically. This not only fosters a sense of community but also provides you with a repository of content that can be repurposed for your marketing efforts.

Negotiating fair terms with influencers is another critical aspect. Remember, while it's important to get a good deal, undervaluing an influencer's worth can harm the partnership. Offer competitive compensation and structure packages that include performance bonuses. Mutual respect and fairness nurtured during negotiations go a long way in maintaining a positive relationship.

One innovative approach gaining traction is influencer takeovers, where an influencer manages your social media account for a day. This not only brings their audience directly to your platform but also provides fresh, engaging content directly from someone your potential customers trust. Just ensure clear guidelines are set to avoid any brand missteps.

Another angle involves affiliate marketing with influencers. This creates ongoing incentives for influencers to promote your products since they earn a commission on each sale referred. This model aligns the interests of both parties and can lead to sustained promotional efforts.

Lastly, always keep the broader picture in mind. Influencer partnerships are just one piece of your marketing strategy. Integrate these efforts with your social media campaigns, email marketing, and even offline activities to create a cohesive, omnichannel strategy. This integrated approach ensures that all your marketing efforts work synergistically, amplifying your reach and impact.

In summary, influencer partnerships are a powerful way to expand your reach and grow your business. Identifying the right influencers, crafting meaningful and authentic campaigns, and maintaining long-term relationships can significantly boost your brand's visibility. With clear objectives, fair negotiations, and innovative strategies, you can harness the influential power of social media personalities to guide your business towards that coveted first $1 million.

Social Media Marketing

Let's start by acknowledging that social media isn't just a passing trend; it's a pivotal tool in your marketing arsenal that can amplify your reach and help you connect with a broader audience. Here's the good news: you don't need a massive budget to make a significant impact. The power of social media lies in creativity, consistency, and engagement.

In the world of entrepreneurship, being active on social media platforms like Facebook, Instagram, Twitter, and LinkedIn can be a game-changer. These platforms offer you a stage to showcase your brand, products, and values. But it's not just about posting content; it's about creating a genuine connection with your audience. Social media allows you to be both personable and professional, offering an excellent balance that can foster trust and loyalty.

Start by identifying which platforms resonate most with your target audience. For instance, LinkedIn may be the most effective for B2B enterprises, while Instagram could be the go-to for lifestyle brands. It's crucial to understand where your potential customers spend most of their time online and invest your efforts there.

Content is king and queen on social media. High-quality, relevant content can set your brand apart from the noise. Whether it's informative blog posts, eye-catching images, or engaging videos, your content should reflect your brand's voice and values. Vary your content types to keep your audience engaged. A diverse content strategy that includes polls, Q&A sessions, behind-the-scenes looks, and customer testimonials can capture and maintain your audience's attention.

Storytelling plays a crucial role in social media marketing. People love stories, especially those they can relate to. Share the story behind your brand, your struggles, and your successes. Authenticity resonates well with audiences. When people see the human side of your business, they feel more connected and are more likely to become loyal customers.

Consistency is another critical factor. Posting sporadically won't cut it. Develop a content calendar to ensure that you're posting regularly. This not only keeps your brand in the spotlight but also lets your audience know that you are active and engaged. Each platform has its own peak times for posting, so do some research to find the best times to post for maximum engagement.

While organic reach is essential, don't underestimate the power of paid advertising on social media. Platforms like Facebook and Instagram offer robust targeting options that allow you to reach specific demographics based on age, location, interests, and behaviors. Experiment with small budget campaigns initially, and optimize them based on the results. Always keep an eye on your ROI to ensure your efforts are paying off.

Engagement is the heartbeat of social media marketing. It isn't enough to post content; you need to interact with your audience. Respond to comments, messages, and mentions. Ask questions to encourage participation, and be sure to acknowledge those who engage with your content. Building a community around your brand can transform casual followers into dedicated advocates.

Influencer marketing can also be a valuable strategy. By partnering with influencers in your niche, you can tap into their follower base and extend your reach. Choose influencers whose values align with your brand, and ensure their followers are your target audience. Authentic collaborations can lead to higher credibility and new customer acquisitions.

Analytics provide insights into what's working and what isn't. Use tools like Facebook Insights, Instagram Analytics, and Twitter Analytics to track your performance. Pay attention to metrics such as engagement rates, click-through rates, and follower growth. Adjust your strategy based on the data to continually improve your efforts.

Cross-promote your social media channels. If you're hosting a giveaway on Instagram, announce it on Twitter and Facebook to drive more traffic. Leveraging multiple platforms can amplify your reach and bring diverse audiences together in one place.

Finally, never stop learning. Social media trends evolve rapidly. Stay updated with the latest changes in algorithms, new features, and emerging platforms. Continuous learning and adaptation will keep you ahead of the curve.

In summary, social media marketing is not a one-size-fits-all approach. It's an ongoing process that requires attention, creativity, and adaptation. By focusing on quality content, engaging with your audience, leveraging analytics, and staying consistent, you can significantly expand your reach and set your business on a path to success.

Chapter 10: Enhancing Customer Experience

Enhancing customer experience is not just about giving your customers what they want – it's about anticipating their needs and exceeding their expectations. Think of this as the spark that turns one-time buyers into loyal advocates for your brand. Start by building efficient feedback loops to capture and analyze customer insights, then implement meaningful changes based on this data. Cultivating loyalty requires genuine engagement and personal touches that can make every transaction feel special. Remember, a happy customer is not just a repeat customer – they're also a powerful marketing tool. Keep your focus on delivering value, being responsive, and maintaining a high standard of service, and watch as your business thrives.

Feedback Loops

Enhancing customer experience isn't just about making a stellar first impression; it's about creating a consistent, ongoing relationship with your customers. One of the most effective tools in your arsenal for achieving this is the feedback loop. Think of a feedback loop as a continuous conversation between you and your customers, where you're not only speaking but also listening and acting upon what you hear.

It's tempting to see customer feedback as a one-off task, a box to be ticked. But if you want to build a million-dollar business, you need to be in perpetual conversation with your customers. A feedback loop allows this conversation to thrive, helping you understand what you're doing right, where you're falling short, and what opportunities you might be missing. You might have a product that's out of this world, but if you're not attuned to what your customers are saying about it, you're leaving money and growth on the table.

The essence of a feedback loop is pretty simple: gather, analyze, and act. But simplicity doesn't always mean easy. The challenge is in the execution. Let's break down each element.

Gather Feedback

First, you need to collect feedback. This isn't always straightforward; people are busy, and getting them to stop and share their thoughts can be like pulling teeth. But it's worth the effort. Use multiple channels: surveys, social media, direct emails, and customer service interactions. Each channel has its own unique advantages. Surveys provide structured data, whereas social media offers real-time, candid insights.

Try to make it as easy as possible for customers to give feedback. A brief, 3-question survey is more likely to get responses than a long, tedious one. Structured questions are great for quantitative analysis, but don't shy away from open-ended questions—they can often provide the most insightful comments.

Analyze Feedback

Once you've gathered feedback, the next step is to analyze it. This isn't just about looking at numbers on a spreadsheet. It's about digging into the nuances of what your customers are saying. For quantitative feedback, tools like Excel or more advanced software like Tableau can help you spot patterns and trends. Qualitative feedback, on the other hand, requires a keen eye and perhaps some natural language processing tools to identify common themes.

The key here is not just identifying what's being said, but also understanding the why behind it. If customers say your website is difficult to navigate, you need to delve deeper. What exactly is causing the frustration? Is it the layout, the loading times, or perhaps an overload of information? The more detailed your analysis, the more effective your subsequent actions will be.

Act on Feedback

CHAPTER 10: ENHANCING CUSTOMER EXPERIENCE

This is where the rubber meets the road. Collecting and analyzing feedback is essential, but it's meaningless if you don't act on it. Prioritize the feedback based on what's most impactful for your customers and feasible for your business. Some changes might be quick wins—tweaks to your website or minor adjustments to your product. Others might require a more significant investment of time and resources.

As you implement changes, communicate them back to your customers. Let them know that you've heard them and are making improvements based on their suggestions. This not only helps to close the loop but also builds trust and reinforces the relationship. Customers appreciate transparency and are more likely to remain loyal if they feel their opinions genuinely matter.

The Continuous Cycle

Remember, feedback loops are continuous. The business landscape evolves, customer preferences shift, and market dynamics change. What works today might not be effective tomorrow. A robust feedback loop keeps you agile and responsive, allowing you to adapt quickly to new challenges and opportunities.

Consider setting up regular review meetings to discuss customer feedback and the actions you're taking. Make this part of your business routine. It's not an afterthought but an integral component of your strategy. Your team should know that customer feedback isn't just something to be dealt with when there's a problem—it's a core driver of your growth and success.

Empowering Your Team

Feedback loops aren't just for the leadership team. Empower your employees to be part of the solution. Customer service representatives, for example, are on the front lines and have a direct pulse on what customers are experiencing. Encourage them to share insights and suggestions. Give them the authority to make minor adjustments on the spot where feasible. This not only speeds up the resolution process but also boosts employee morale and engagement.

Moreover, involve different departments in the feedback loop process. When marketing hears directly from customers, they can tailor their messaging more effectively. When product development understands customer pain points, they can innovate solutions that truly meet market needs. In short, make feedback everyone's business.

Feedback Loops in the Digital Age

The digital age offers unprecedented opportunities for creating robust feedback loops. Leverage technology to gather and analyze feedback more efficiently. Tools like CRM systems, social media monitoring platforms, and customer feedback software can provide valuable insights and streamline the process.

Automation can also play a role. For example, automated follow-up emails after a purchase can solicit feedback while the experience is still fresh in the customer's mind. Chatbots can handle initial inquiries and collect preliminary feedback, which can later be analyzed by human agents. However, don't rely solely on automation—personal touchpoints are still invaluable.

Closing the Loop

Closing the loop isn't just about making changes; it's about showing your customers that their voices make a difference. This means going back to them, explaining what changes were made, and thanking them for their input. Whether through email updates, social media announcements, or blog posts, keep your customers in the loop about how their feedback is shaping your business.

You can even spotlight customers who've made particularly valuable suggestions. This not only reinforces that you're listening but also builds a community of engaged and loyal customers. People love to feel appreciated, and a simple thanks can go a long way.

Feedback to Feed Forward

Finally, think of feedback not just as a way to correct mistakes but as a source of new ideas and opportunities. Some of the best innovations come from listening to what customers have to say. They might point out an entirely new market need or suggest a feature you hadn't considered. In this way, your feedback loop becomes a feed-forward loop, continually propelling your business toward greater growth and innovation.

Feedback loops are the backbone of enhancing customer experience. They keep your business grounded in reality, attuned to your customers' needs, and agile enough to respond to changes. Make it a priority, embed it into your culture, and watch how this simple yet powerful tool can guide you to your first $1 million and beyond.

Building Customer Loyalty

Enhancing customer experience isn't just about immediate satisfaction; it's about fostering long-term relationships that keep customers coming back. This brings us to the critical goal of building customer loyalty. Think about it—once you've gotten someone to buy from you, the real challenge is ensuring they return. Why spend loads of money on acquiring new customers when you can get more value from the ones you already have? Loyal customers are not just repeat buyers; they're your brand advocates, your unpaid marketing team. But how do you get there?

First, let's talk about the basics: delivering consistent value. It might sound obvious, but consistently meeting or exceeding customer expectations sets the stage for loyalty. Every interaction a customer has with your brand should reinforce their decision to choose you over the competition. Whether it's through exceptional product quality, superior customer service, or a user-friendly experience, your goal is to make customers feel they've made the right choice.

Know your customers. Understanding their preferences, needs, and behaviors can help you tailor your products and services in a way that resonates with them. Use data analytics to gather insights but don't underestimate the power of a personal touch. Personalized emails, exclusive offers, and special services make customers feel understood and valued. The sense of belonging to an exclusive club can be incredibly powerful.

Another strategy is building a community around your brand. This can be as simple as creating a vibrant social media presence or as complex as hosting events and webinars. When customers feel part of a community, they're more likely to stick around. Build forums or engage via platforms like Facebook and Instagram where people can share their own experiences with your products. Fostering a sense of belonging and mutual support strengthens the emotional connection between the customer and your brand.

Transparency and honesty go a long way in building trust, which is the bedrock of customer loyalty. If something goes wrong, own up to it. Address customer complaints efficiently and honestly. Surprisingly, handling errors effectively can strengthen loyalty more than a flawless transaction. Customers appreciate knowing a company is willing to correct mistakes and values their input.

Loyalty programs can also be remarkably effective, but they need to be meaningful and straightforward. People are busy; they don't want to jump through hoops to earn a reward. Points-based systems, tiered rewards, and referral incentives are all popular options. The key here is to design a program that truly adds value and is easy to understand.

Customer feedback is a goldmine for insights and improvements. Regularly solicit feedback, and more importantly, act on it. Whether through surveys, reviews, or social media comments, knowing what your customers think can help you refine your strategies. Customers who feel heard are more likely to feel loyal to your brand.

Social proof and testimonials can also amplify loyalty. Positive reviews and case studies showcasing satisfied customers reassure potential buyers and reinforce existing customers' faith in your brand. Don't be shy about asking loyal customers to share their experiences; most people are happy to help a brand they love.

The power of surprise can't be underestimated. Unexpected perks or gifts can create memorable experiences that foster loyalty. This could be something as small as a handwritten thank-you note or as big as a surprise discount. These small acts of appreciation can leave a lasting impression.

Education is another underutilized tool in building loyalty. Sharing knowledge through blogs, tutorials, or online courses not only positions you as an industry leader but also adds value beyond your core product. When customers see you as more than just a seller—when they view you as a valuable resource—they're more likely to stay loyal.

Offering exemplary customer service is akin to rolling out the red carpet for your customers. Prompt responses, efficient problem resolution, and going above and beyond can turn casual customers into loyal fans. Train your customer service team to treat each interaction as an opportunity to strengthen the customer relationship.

Finally, keep an eye on competitors, but don't mimic them. Stand out by offering unique value that they can't replicate. Whether it's through innovation, superior quality, or exceptional service, make sure you offer something distinct.

In summary, building customer loyalty is a multifaceted process that demands consistent effort and a genuine commitment to your customers. By providing consistent value, understanding your customers on a personal level, building a community, maintaining transparency, offering meaningful loyalty programs, soliciting feedback, showcasing social proof, surprising your customers, educating them, delivering exemplary customer service, and offering unique value, you'll be well on your way to creating a loyal customer base that supports you not just through your first million, but for years to come.

Chapter 11: Financial Management

Managing your finances effectively is the backbone of any successful business. A solid financial plan not only keeps your operations smooth but also prepares you for unexpected challenges. You'll need to master budgeting for growth, so you're investing wisely in areas that will yield high returns without overextending your resources. Cash flow management is another critical aspect—it ensures you have the capital on hand to meet your obligations and seize new opportunities as they arise. By developing a keen sense of how money moves through your business, you'll be better equipped to make strategic decisions that fuel your journey toward that first $1 million.

Budgeting for Growth

When you're scaling up a business, one of the most crucial aspects to consider is budgeting for growth. Growth doesn't come without its costs, and this section is designed to help you navigate the complex financial landscape that expansion brings. The aim is to make sure your financial management strategy is robust enough to withstand the pressures of scaling while still giving you the flexibility to seize new opportunities.

First things first: assess your current financial situation. Look at your earnings, expenditures, and profit margins. Understanding where you stand today will give you a solid foundation upon which to build. Too many entrepreneurs dive headfirst into growth without a clear picture of their financial health, which often leads to pitfalls and setbacks. Use tools like financial statements, balance sheets, and cash flow statements to get a clear snapshot.

Next, you'll want to create a growth budget that's realistic yet ambitious. The goal here is to find a balance where your budget supports your growth without risking the financial stability of your business. Start with the basics: projected income, fixed costs, and variable expenses. Factor in the costs of marketing campaigns, product development, and potential hires. But don't forget to set aside a contingency fund for unexpected expenses. They will come up; it's just a matter of when.

When you're allocating funds, prioritize investments that will generate revenue quickly. The idea is to create a cycle where initial investments generate returns that can be reinvested into further growth. For example, marketing and advertising campaigns that bring in new customers should be high on your list. However, be cautious about spending too much too fast. A sudden influx of cash can sometimes lead to reckless spending, which is a sure path to financial strain.

Now, let's talk about leveraging technology to manage your budget effectively. Tools like budgeting software and financial management apps can provide real-time insights into your financial status. Software such as QuickBooks, Xero, and FreshBooks can be invaluable. They allow you to track expenses, categorize them, and analyze spending patterns. This data can help you make informed decisions about where to cut costs and where to invest more.

While technology is important, don't underestimate the value of human expertise. Consider hiring a financial advisor or a part-time CFO, especially if numbers aren't your strong suit. These professionals can provide insights that you might overlook and help you create a financial strategy that's aligned with your growth objectives.

Understanding the concept of "burn rate" is also essential. Your burn rate is the rate at which you are spending money before you're profitable. Keeping this in check is critical for long-term sustainability. Regularly review your burn rate in the context of your revenue growth. If expenses are growing faster than income, it's a red flag that needs immediate attention.

Another vital component of budgeting for growth is debt management. While taking on some debt can be beneficial for financing growth, make sure it's manageable. Don't let debt accumulate to a point where it hampers your ability to reinvest in the business. Be aware of interest rates and the repayment timelines. Assess if your projected revenue will cover these costs and leave room for profitability.

Cash flow management should never be an afterthought. In fact, effective cash flow management is the backbone of successful financial management. A positive cash flow ensures that you have the resources to cover your operational expenses, invest in growth opportunities, and cushion against unexpected financial downturns. Forecast your cash flow regularly and adjust your budget to reflect any changes.

Consider diversifying your income streams. Relying on a single source of income can be risky. Think about how you can add new revenue streams that align with your existing business model. This could be new products, services, or even entering new markets. Diversification can provide a more stable financial foundation and reduce risks associated with market fluctuations.

It's worth exploring external funding options if your growth ambitions outpace what your existing revenue can support. Venture capital, angel investors, and even crowdfunding platforms can provide the financial boost needed to scale quickly. However, these options come with their own set of pros and cons, including equity dilution and increased financial scrutiny. Weigh these carefully before making a decision.

Regularly review and adjust your growth budget. The business landscape is dynamic, and what worked a few months ago may not be as effective today. Schedule monthly or quarterly reviews to assess your financial performance against your growth goals. Use these insights to tweak your budget, allocate resources more effectively, and stay on track.

Don't neglect the importance of building financial reserves. A healthy reserve can act as a safety net for your business. It's your backup plan for when things don't go as expected. Aim to build reserves that can cover at least six months' worth of operational expenses. This may sound daunting, but it's a crucial part of resilient financial planning.

Lastly, foster a culture of financial discipline within your team. Everyone in your organization should understand the importance of budgeting and financial responsibility. Encourage teams to be mindful of their expenditures and look for cost-effective solutions. This collective effort can go a long way in maintaining financial health as you grow.

Budgeting for growth isn't just about crunching numbers; it's about creating a strategic plan that aligns with your vision and goals. By being diligent, making informed decisions, and leveraging both technology and human expertise, you can set the stage for sustainable growth. Remember, it's a balance between ambition and pragmatism that will ultimately determine your success.

Cash Flow Management

Cash flow management is the lifeblood of any successful business. It's not just about knowing how much money is coming in; it's also about understanding where it's going out and how to optimize that process. The goal is to ensure that your business always has enough capital to meet its obligations while investing in growth opportunities. Mismanagement here can spell disaster, but done right, it can pave the way to your first $1 million.

At its core, cash flow management involves tracking all sources of revenue and all outgoing expenses. This may sound simple, but the complexity ramps up as your business grows. Each dollar that comes into your business must be carefully accounted for and used purposefully, whether it's reinvested into marketing, used to pay salaries, or allocated to operational costs. Businesses that manage to balance these elements effectively are the ones that thrive in both the short and long term.

Understanding your cash flow starts with generating accurate financial reports. These include income statements, balance sheets, and cash flow statements. These documents are not just for your accountant; they should be tools you use frequently. By analyzing these reports, you'll gain insights into trends and patterns that can inform better decision-making. You'll know when you're likely to face a cash crunch and can prepare accordingly.

Timing is crucial in cash flow management. Knowing when your big bills are due and when your revenue flows in can help you avoid any gaps. Sometimes, the gap between expenditures and incoming cash can be bridged with short-term financing options like lines of credit. Having these options available can mean the difference between making payroll or missing it.

It's also essential to differentiate between profits and cash flow. A business might show a profit on paper but still face cash flow challenges if revenues are tied up in receivables or inventory. Regularly review your accounts receivable and encourage timely payments from your customers. Offering small discounts for early payments can incentivize quicker cash inflow, easing potential cash flow constraints.

Equally important is managing your payables smartly. Negotiate longer payment terms with your suppliers without ruining relationships. This may give you a bit more time to get cash into your pocket before you need to spend it again. It's a delicate balance, requiring good business relationships and excellent negotiation skills.

Automation can also be a game-changer in cash flow management. Utilizing software that tracks and manages invoices, reminders, and payments can save time and reduce errors. This kind of technology can provide real-time insights into your cash flow status, allowing you to make informed decisions quickly.

Risk management plays a significant role in cash flow management. What if a major client delays their payment? What if an unexpected expense pops up? Having a reserve fund can act as a buffer against these unforeseen events. Aim to have at least three to six months of operating expenses saved so your business can navigate through rough patches without significant disruptions.

Remember that sound cash flow management also involves knowing when to cut costs and when to invest. Regularly review all your expenses to identify areas where you can trim the fat. Sometimes cutting seemingly small expenses can add up to significant savings over time. On the flip side, knowing when to invest in growth opportunities can propel your business forward.

Profit margins and cash flow, while interrelated, require separate strategies

CHAPTER 11: FINANCIAL MANAGEMENT

to optimize. Increasing your prices can boost your cash flow, but it requires careful market analysis and customer communication. Conversely, reducing costs without sacrificing quality can also have a substantial positive impact on your cash reserves.

For ambitious entrepreneurs aiming for that first million, one critical aspect is the timing of investments. Launching new products or expanding into new markets requires capital. Proper cash flow management ensures that you have the financial flexibility to seize these growth opportunities without jeopardizing your day-to-day operations.

Don't overlook the importance of comprehensive budgeting. A well-crafted budget allows you to forecast revenues and expenses accurately, offering a roadmap for your financial future. Regularly compare your actual performance against your budget to spot any discrepancies early and adjust your strategies where necessary.

Strategic planning is another cornerstone. Projecting your cash flow for future periods—monthly, quarterly, and yearly—can identify potential shortfalls well in advance. This kind of foresight enables strategic adjustments, such as delaying a non-essential purchase or accelerating a marketing campaign to boost sales.

Moreover, one-on-one consultations with financial experts can provide valuable insights tailored to your specific business needs. Many entrepreneurs make the mistake of trying to handle everything themselves. Sometimes, it's worth investing in expert advice to help navigate complex financial landscapes, offering peace of mind and strategic clarity.

Cash flow management isn't just about the present; it's also about preparing for the future. As your business grows, so will your expenses and revenue streams. Continually refine your cash flow strategies to accommodate this growth. Regularly update your financial models and reassess your cash flow statements to ensure they remain accurate as your business evolves.

On a more practical note, always prepare for tax obligations. Set aside a portion of your profits in a separate account designated explicitly for taxes. This ensures you won't be caught off-guard when tax season rolls around, safeguarding both your liquidity and your peace of mind.

Finally, fostering a cash flow-positive culture within your organization can be transformative. Educate your team on the importance of cash flow and involve them in decision-making processes that impact it. When everyone understands the significance of maintaining a healthy cash flow, you're more likely to achieve coordinated, effective solutions.

In conclusion, strong cash flow management is indispensable for reaching your first $1 million. It requires constant vigilance, proactive planning, and a willingness to adapt. By mastering the art of cash flow management, you'll lay down a solid financial foundation that supports not just growth, but also long-term sustainability for your business.

Chapter 12: The Gold (Months 9-12)

Now that you've got the ball rolling, it's time to dive into the gold—literally. These final months are all about harnessing momentum and expanding your offerings to secure long-term success. You've set the stage for your initial product; now, think bigger. Start by establishing a product series to cater to different segments of your audience. Diversification is key. Implement new versions, complementary products, or creative bundles to broaden your market appeal. This is your chance to ask, "What's next?" and act on it decisively. As you roll out these new offerings, keep an eye on customer feedback and market trends. Adjust, pivot, and innovate as needed. Remember, this phase isn't just about boosting sales; it's about cementing your brand's presence in a competitive market. The efforts you put in now will lay the groundwork for sustaining 100 sales per day, making those future growth milestones not only achievable but inevitable. Prepare yourself to turn ambition into action and watch as your venture reaches new heights.

Establishing a Product Series

Welcome to the golden months of your entrepreneurial journey, where the foundation you've laid and the growth you've fostered start to bear tangible rewards. It's now time to level up. Establishing a product series isn't just a suggestion; it's a strategy that will catapult your business into a new realm of profitability and market share. But what does creating a product series entail, and how can you do it effectively?

Firstly, think of a product series as a family of products that complement each other. These are items that not only appeal to your existing customers but also attract new ones. The idea here is to build an ecosystem around your brand, one where customers feel compelled to buy multiple products because they work so well together. Consider Apple, how their products – iPhone, MacBook, iPad – are designed to work seamlessly with each other. Your goal is to achieve the same kind of synergy within your product line.

Now, let's break down the practical steps you need to take to establish a successful product series.

Begin by analyzing your current product and understanding your customer's journey. What are the natural next steps for someone who purchases your product? For instance, if you're selling fitness equipment, consider what other items would enhance the user's experience: supplements, workout gear, or even training programs. Customer feedback and market research will give you invaluable insights into these opportunities.

Developing complementary products doesn't mean straying far from your core offering. In fact, you should aim to deepen your current positioning. When customers trust your brand for one quality product, they're more likely to buy another. This means the new products must maintain or exceed the quality and consistency of your original offering. Imagine you've built a reputation for high-quality running shoes; now is the perfect time to introduce related products like running apparel or sports accessories without diluting your brand's core competency.

Next, focus on modularity and versatility. The best product series offer scalability; your customers should be able to add new products to their collection without additional hassle. Each product should serve an independent function but work better together in a set. For example, a skincare line could include cleansers, toners, and moisturizers that are effective on their own but provide enhanced benefits when used in a sequence.

Consider tiered pricing as you expand your product line. By offering products at different price points, you widen your customer base. Your premium versions appeal to high-end buyers, while more affordable options attract budget-conscious consumers. This approach can also introduce customers to your brand with a lower-priced item, increasing the likelihood

CHAPTER 12: THE GOLD (MONTHS 9-12)

they'll purchase higher-end products in the future.

Marketing plays a crucial role in establishing a successful product series. It's imperative to maintain consistent branding across your entire product line. Your marketing materials should highlight how the new products complement the original ones and enhance the overall user experience. Use storytelling to connect with your audience; show them how each new product fits into the broader narrative of your brand.

Another crucial aspect is leveraging your current customers. Your existing client base is your low-hanging fruit; they already love and trust your brand. Use email marketing, social media campaigns, and exclusive offers to introduce them to your new products. Implement loyalty programs or bundling options to encourage multiple purchases. For instance, a "complete home office setup" bundle might include a desk, chair, and ergonomic accessories, offering both convenience and a discount.

Partnerships can also be invaluable. Collaborate with influencers and other brands to co-create products or promote your series. This not only broadens your reach but also adds a layer of credibility. For instance, if you're selling organic food products, partnering with a popular nutritionist or celebrity chef for a co-branded product can skyrocket your sales.

Don't overlook the power of limited editions and exclusivity. Limited edition products create urgency and can significantly boost sales. People love the idea of owning something exclusive. These products can be seasonal or event-based, adding a "collectible" aspect to your brand which encourages repeat purchases.

It's also important to continuously iterate based on feedback and performance metrics. Monitor key performance indicators (KPIs) such as sales numbers, customer reviews, and return rates. Regularly updating your product series based on real customer data ensures you're meeting their evolving needs and preferences.

Finally, invest in scalable operational capabilities. As your product line expands, your logistics, customer support, and inventory management systems need to keep pace. Efficiently managing multiple products requires robust systems that can seamlessly handle everything from sourcing materials to delivering the final product to your customers' doorsteps.

By now, you should clearly understand that establishing a product series is not just about adding more items to your inventory; it's about creating a cohesive ecosystem that magnifies the value of each individual product. You're building an interconnected portfolio that makes it easier for your customers to keep engaging with your brand, increasing their lifetime value and your bottom line.

These golden months are about taking calculated risks and making well-informed decisions to ensure your product series resonates with your audience. Remember, the ultimate goal is to create a product line so compelling that your customers keep coming back for more, driving you towards that coveted $1 million milestone.

With a well-thought-out product series, you're not just selling products; you're building a legacy. Your brand becomes synonymous with quality, value, and innovation. The sky's the limit from here. Happy creating!

Diversifying Your Offerings

Diversifying your offerings is not just an option; it's a necessity for sustainable growth, especially in the crucial months from 9 to 12, also known as "The Gold." This period is where you've got some solid traction, and now it's about multiplying your avenues for revenue. Diversification is the key to stability and long-term success.

First, let's explore why diversification is so essential. Think of it this way: relying on a single product is like walking a tightrope without a safety net. If something were to go wrong, you'd have no backup plan. Markets fluctuate, customer preferences change, and unforeseen issues like supply chain disruptions or new competitors can derail your plans. By adding more offerings, you're essentially creating multiple safety nets. Diversification protects your business from being overly dependent on one stream of income.

So, how do you go about it? The first step is understanding the core competencies of your business and how they can be extended into new areas. Look at your existing products. What are the features or aspects that your customers love the most? Once you've pinpointed these features, think about how they can be tweaked or re-packaged into new products or services. This could be as simple as introducing variations of your current product, such as different sizes, colors, or bundles, or as complex as launching entirely new product lines.

Another effective way to diversify is to analyze your customer data. Who are your top buyers? What do they have in common? Utilize customer feedback and data analytics to identify additional needs or problems that you can solve. For example, if you're selling home fitness equipment, perhaps your customers would also be interested in online fitness classes, nutritional supplements, or workout apparel. These complementary products not only meet diverse customer needs but also build a more comprehensive brand ecosystem.

Consider entering new markets as well. This doesn't necessarily mean going global (although it could), but rather exploring niche markets within your current demographic. Sometimes, a slight adjustment to your marketing message or product features can make your offering more appealing to a different segment of your audience. Don't underestimate the power of niche markets; they can be incredibly loyal and lucrative.

Collaborations and partnerships are another powerful way to diversify your offerings. Teaming up with other brands or influencers in your industry can introduce your products to a broader audience while also providing added value to your existing customers. For instance, if you're in the tech space, partnering with a software company can bring a new dimension to your hardware products through bundled deals.

Now, let's talk about digital products and services, which are incredibly versatile. Whether it's eBooks, online courses, or subscription models, these offerings can complement your physical products nicely. Digital products often have the added benefit of lower production costs and can be scaled more easily. Plus, they offer another point of engagement with your customer base, keeping them involved with your brand.

You also might want to diversify by expanding your sales channels. If you've been primarily selling online, consider adding physical retail options, pop-up shops, or participating in trade shows. Conversely, if you're already in brick-and-mortar stores, now might be the time to invest in an eCommerce platform, if you haven't already. Each of these channels opens up new customer bases and revenue streams.

Another critical approach is to leverage seasonal trends and events. Depending on your industry, there will be particular times of the year when demand naturally spikes. By creating specialized product lines or limited-time offers tailored to these times, you can capture additional sales. Think about holiday-themed products, back-to-school supplies, or summer vacation gear. Seasonal diversification helps keep your brand fresh and relevant all year round.

Financial investments in your diversification efforts should also be strategic. Allocate a portion of your budget to researching and developing new products. Always keep some resources aside for marketing these new offerings. Your primary goal should be to ensure these new products resonate well with your existing customer base while also attracting new customers.

Even as you diversify, maintaining high-quality standards is paramount. Expanding too quickly or compromising on quality can dilute your brand and alienate your customer base. Always ensure that any new product or service you offer undergoes rigorous testing and quality control. Customer trust is hard-earned and easily lost.

Lastly, let's touch on the psychological and motivational aspects of diversification. Diversifying your offerings can reinvigorate your team and add excitement to your business. It breaks the monotony and encourages innovation and creativity within your organization. When employees see that the company is expanding and exploring new horizons, it often boosts morale and engagement.

In conclusion, the journey from 9 to 12 months into your business is a pivotal time to diversify your offerings. Whether it's through new product lines, expanded services, strategic partnerships, or entering new markets, the end goal is to build a resilient business. Remember, diversification isn't about changing your business; it's about adding layers to it. By offering a variety of products and services, you not only create multiple streams of revenue but

CHAPTER 12: THE GOLD (MONTHS 9-12)

also build a brand that can withstand market fluctuations and stand the test of time. So, take those calculated risks, invest in innovation, and watch your business flourish.

Chapter 13: Sustaining 100 Sales Per Day

You've hit 25 sales per day, and you're on a roll—great job! Now, let's talk about taking it up a notch and sustaining 100 sales per day. This is where things get serious, and you need to bring out the advanced sales techniques. Think strategically about loyalty programs; they can turn occasional buyers into regular customers. Keep refining your approach by using data-driven insights to identify what's working and drop what isn't. Automation tools can help you streamline without sacrificing personal touch. Remember, consistency is key here—maintain the quality of your product and customer service to ensure repeat business. Staying agile and continuously improving based on customer feedback will help keep your sales numbers steady. If you focus on building strong relationships with your customers and delivering exceptional value, you'll be well on your way to maintaining those 100 sales per day.

Advanced Sales Techniques

Let's dive into the nitty-gritty of advanced sales techniques—because let's face it, getting to 100 sales per day isn't just about throwing spaghetti at the wall and seeing what sticks. It's about consistency, innovation, and yes, a bit of strategy.

First off, prioritize personalization. Understanding your customers on a deeper level can make a world of difference. Personalization goes beyond just slapping their name in an email subject line. Use data analytics to gain insights into their behaviors, preferences, and pain points. Then tailor your communication, offers, and customer journey around that data. This isn't a nice-to-have; it's a must-have. You want your customer to feel like you're speaking directly to them, solving their unique problems, and anticipating their needs.

Next, let's talk about leveraging psychological triggers. Humans are emotional beings, and certain psychological triggers can positively influence their buying decisions. Scarcity and urgency are classics, but what about social proof and authority? Showcase testimonials, customer reviews, and case studies. Get industry experts to endorse your product. Trust is hard-earned but worth every bit of effort.

Don't underestimate the power of storytelling. Your product isn't just a product—it's a solution, a hero in someone's journey. Craft compelling stories around your brand and product. Share customer success stories that showcase transformation, and make those stories relatable. Simple facts tell, but stories sell. It's an age-old adage because it's true. Stories connect emotionally, breaking down barriers and fostering loyalty.

Another advanced sales technique revolves around upselling and cross-selling. If you've ever ordered a burger and been asked if you'd like fries with that, you've been cross-sold to. If they've suggested making it a combo for a little extra, you've been upsold to. Learn your product catalog inside and out and find natural pairings that complement each purchase. Position these upsells and cross-sells as value-added options. Your goal is to genuinely enhance the customer's experience and satisfaction, not just to inflate your bottom line.

Let's shift gears to automation. While it might seem counterintuitive to talk about automation when discussing personalization, it's not. Automations can handle those repetitive tasks, freeing you up to focus on the strategic aspects of sales. Automated emails, chatbots, and CRM systems can track and nurture leads without constant manual input. The key is to set them up thoughtfully and ensure they're seamlessly integrated into your overall customer experience. Properly executed, automation can enhance personalization by ensuring timely, relevant communication.

Quality over quantity is crucial when it comes to leads. Not all potential customers are created equal, and spending time chasing uninterested leads is inefficient. Implement lead scoring to prioritize the hottest prospects. This system ranks leads based on interest level, engagement, and how well they fit your ideal customer profile. Focus your efforts on leads with the highest likelihood of conversion. This is a technique that saves time and enhances conversion rates.

Mastering negotiation tactics is also vital. The art of negotiation goes beyond just price. It's about value and perception. Equip your sales team with strategies to handle objections seamlessly. Train them to communicate value effectively and understand when to compromise. A well-negotiated sale can lead to repeat business and referrals, while a poorly handled negotiation can sour potential long-term relationships.

Incorporate multi-channel strategies into your sales plan. Don't rely solely on one avenue for sales. Diversify your approach through different platforms—email marketing, social media, online marketplaces, and even traditional methods like phone calls and face-to-face interactions, if relevant. The idea is to be where your customers are, providing multiple touchpoints and enhancing the likelihood of conversion.

Work on building partnerships and collaborations. Collaboration with other businesses can open doors to new customer bases that you might not reach otherwise. Find synergies with complementary businesses and create joint offers, bundles, or even co-branded content. It's a win-win situation that can exponentially increase your reach and sales.

Experimentation is a fantastic tool. Don't be afraid to test new approaches, whether it's in your sales pitch, your marketing channels, or even your product lineup. Implement A/B testing to compare the effectiveness of different strategies. Track performance metrics rigorously and be prepared to pivot based on data. Flexibility and willingness to adapt can position you miles ahead of competitors stuck in their ways.

Next up is focusing on repeat customers. It's significantly easier and more cost-effective to retain existing customers than it is to acquire new ones. Implement loyalty programs that reward repeat business and foster a sense of community around your brand. Offer exclusive deals, early access to new products, and personalized perks for your best customers. Essentially, make them feel special and appreciated.

Finally, invest in continuous learning and training for your sales team. The landscape is ever-evolving, and what worked yesterday might not work tomorrow. Equip your team with the latest tools, techniques, and insights. Encourage them to share their experiences, successes, and challenges. A well-trained, motivated team will always outperform one that's stuck in a rut.

In summary, advanced sales techniques are your bread and butter for scaling to and sustaining 100 sales per day. Focus on personalization, leverage psychological triggers, and tell compelling stories. Don't underestimate the power of upselling and cross-selling, and remember that automation, when done right, can enhance your customer interactions. Prioritize quality leads, master negotiation tactics, and embrace multi-channel strategies. Forge powerful partnerships, continuously experiment, nurture your repeat customers, and invest in training your team. These techniques, when woven together, create a robust framework capable of driving and sustaining high sales volumes.

Loyalty Programs

To sustain 100 sales per day, leveraging loyalty programs is an incredibly effective strategy. These programs do much more than just drive repeat business; they foster a sense of community and engagement that aligns customers with your brand's ethos. Think of them as the glue that binds your growing customer base to your business, ensuring that they not only come back but do so with increased frequency and enthusiasm.

Loyalty programs can take various forms, from points systems to tiered memberships. The beauty of these programs lies in their flexibility and adaptability to suit almost any business model. One of the foundational elements is to ensure that the rewards are attractive and achievable. If customers feel they have to spend an enormous amount to gain a reward, they're likely to be disillusioned and disengage. Balance is key. Offer rewards that are valuable yet reachable.

The simplest form of a loyalty program is the points system. Customers earn points for each purchase, which they can later redeem for discounts, free products, or special services. This can be set up easily with an e-commerce platform or POS system that allows for integration of such features. For example, a customer earns one point per dollar spent and can redeem 100 points for a $10 discount. It's straightforward, easy to understand, and highly effective in keeping your customers coming back.

On the more sophisticated side, consider a tiered loyalty program. In this structure, customers ascend through different levels based on their spending or engagement, each tier offering better rewards than the previous. For instance, a 'Silver' tier might offer a 5% discount, while a 'Gold' tier offers 10%, plus early access to new products. This not only incentivizes customers to spend more but also makes them feel part of an exclusive group, enhancing brand loyalty and fostering a deeper connection.

Personalization is another powerful element you can't ignore. Tailor rewards to individual preferences and past purchasing behaviors for an added layer of customer satisfaction. If you know a customer regularly buys skincare products, offer them a free sample of the latest serum when they join your loyalty program or reach a certain spending threshold. CRM software can be invaluable here. Utilize it to track customer behavior and send personalized offers that resonate on a personal level.

Communication is vital for the success of any loyalty program. Keep your customers informed about their points, available rewards, and exclusive offers. An email newsletter can be an effective way to do this. Moreover, don't overlook the power of SMS. Many customers appreciate instant notifications about their rewards balance or alerts for special promotions. Make sure your communication channels are as efficient and user-friendly as possible.

Remember also to create moments of delight beyond the expected rewards. Anniversaries, birthdays, or even a simple thank-you note can go a long way in making customers feel valued. Small, unexpected surprises can cement their loyalty and differentiate your brand from the competition. Think of how Netflix occasionally sends personalized recommendations. It's the small, thoughtful gestures that create an emotional connection with the brand.

Tracking the success of your loyalty programs is crucial. Use analytics to measure customer retention rates, basket sizes, and engagement levels. Are customers in your loyalty program spending more? Are they more likely to recommend your brand? These insights will help you fine-tune your strategy, ensuring that your program is both engaging and effective.

Additionally, it's essential to advertise your loyalty program effectively. Utilize your marketing channels to inform potential and existing customers about the benefits and how easy it is to join. A well-placed banner on your website, posts on social media, and in-store materials can significantly boost enrollments. Consider launching a limited-time incentive for joining, such as an extra bonus point offer or a small gift.

Don't forget to leverage psychological triggers. People love to be part of something bigger than themselves. Highlight the community aspect of your loyalty program. Share stories of top-tier members, showcase behind-the-scenes content, or organize exclusive events. This helps in creating a sense of belonging among your customers.

Incentivizing behaviors other than purchases is another strategy to consider. Points for reviews, social media shares, or referrals can bring multiple advantages. Not only does this make customers feel more engaged with your brand, but it also extends your marketing reach. A customer who shares their recent purchase on Instagram earns points and promotes your brand to their followers at the same time.

One challenge you may encounter is maintaining interest over the long term. If a loyalty program feels stale or unexciting, customer engagement will diminish. Regular updates and new ways to earn and redeem points can keep the program fresh. Seasonal promotions, limited-time offers, and exclusive previews of upcoming products are excellent tactics to maintain enthusiasm.

Lastly, consider partnering with complementary brands to expand the scope of your loyalty program. If you run a coffee shop, for instance, partnering with a local bookstore for joint promotions can enrich the customer experience while introducing your brand to new audiences. Collaborative efforts can make your program more attractive and versatile, boosting its appeal and effectiveness.

In summary, a well-structured and effectively communicated loyalty program can be a game-changer in your journey to sustaining 100 sales per day. Variants like points systems, tiered memberships, personalized offers, and cross-promotional partnerships add multiple dimensions to the experience. Measurement and adaptability ensure the program evolves with your customer base, keeping it engaging and valuable.

Chapter 14: Automating Your Business

It's time to think about how you can buy back your most valuable asset: time. Automation is the secret sauce that lets you do more with less, and today's technology makes it easier than ever. Start by identifying repetitive tasks that consume your day, from customer service emails to inventory management, and consider using software solutions to handle these for you. Don't forget about outsourcing; delegating tasks to remote teams or freelancers can be a game-changer. The key is to streamline operations so you can focus on what truly matters—scaling your business and innovating new pathways to success. Embrace automation, and you'll create a self-sustaining machine that propels you towards that $1 million milestone and beyond.

Leveraging Technology

Embracing technology isn't just about having the latest gizmo or app; it's about weaving it seamlessly into the fabric of your business operations to eliminate inefficiencies, scale effectively, and amplify your capabilities. In today's digital age, leveraging technology lies at the heart of automating your business, enabling you to focus on innovation and growth rather than getting bogged down by mundane tasks.

Start with the basics: your day-to-day operations. Integrating simple software solutions can streamline processes that are typically time-consuming. For instance, accounting software like QuickBooks or Xero automates your financial tasks, from invoicing to payroll, freeing up hours of administrative work. No more manual data entry or reconciliations—just clean, accurate records at your fingertips.

Next, customer relationship management (CRM) systems like Salesforce or HubSpot can revolutionize how you interact with customers. These platforms consolidate customer information, track interactions, and manage follow-ups efficiently. Automated email sequences, personalized responses, and lead scoring features ensure you're always engaging with your audience in a timely manner, turning potential leads into loyal customers.

Automation also extends to your marketing efforts. Tools like Hootsuite and Buffer allow you to schedule social media posts across various platforms. Consistent, strategic posts keep your audience engaged without the need for daily manual updates. Coupled with analytics provided by these tools, you gain insights into what content works best, refining your strategy for maximum engagement.

When it comes to email marketing, platforms like Mailchimp or ConvertKit enable you to create automated email campaigns tailored to different segments of your audience. Welcome emails, drip campaigns, and cart abandonment reminders are just the tip of the iceberg. These automated workflows ensure consistent communication and nurture leads through the sales funnel, enhancing your chances of conversion.

For e-commerce businesses, leveraging technology can significantly simplify operations. Platforms like Shopify, WooCommerce, or BigCommerce handle inventory management, order processing, and customer service seamlessly. Integrate them with inventory management tools like TradeGecko or Stitch Labs, and you have a real-time view of stock levels, helping to avoid overselling or stockouts.

Then there's the power of artificial intelligence (AI) and machine learning. AI chatbots, for instance, provide customer support around the clock, answering queries and guiding users through their purchasing journey. This not only enhances customer satisfaction but also reduces the need for a large customer service team. Platforms like Drift or Intercom make implementing AI chatbots straightforward, with customizable features to suit your business needs.

Automating your supply chain and logistics can also have a profound impact on your business. Software like Oracle NetSuite or SAP automates order tracking, supplier management, and inventory restocking, ensuring a smooth flow of goods from manufacturer to customer. This level of automation minimizes delays, reduces errors, and keeps your operations running like a well-oiled machine.

On the backend, leveraging technology for project management and team collaboration is crucial. Tools like Asana, Trello, or Slack create a centralized hub where teams can track projects, assign tasks, and communicate efficiently. Automated reminders for deadlines, progress tracking, and transparent workflows ensure everyone is aligned and productive.

Data is the lifeblood of any modern business, and leveraging technology for data analytics can provide significant insights. Tools like Google Analytics, Tableau, or Power BI help you visualize data, identify trends, and make informed decisions. Automated data collection and reporting save time and provide a clear picture of your business's performance, guiding your strategic initiatives.

Security shouldn't be an afterthought when leveraging technology. Automating your cybersecurity measures with tools like Norton or McAfee ensures continuous monitoring for threats, automatic updates, and real-time alerts. Protecting your business from cyber threats must be a priority, and appropriate technologies can safeguard sensitive data without constant manual oversight.

For those involved in content creation, leveraging technology for automation can be a game-changer. Platforms like Canva, Adobe Creative Cloud, or even smaller tools like Grammarly automate tedious aspects of content creation and editing. These tools enable you to produce professional-quality content quickly and efficiently, upholding your brand's image without draining resources.

With all these technological tools at your disposal, it's crucial to ensure they're integrated efficiently. Platforms like Zapier or Integromat act as bridges between various software applications, enabling them to communicate and share data seamlessly. Automated workflows created through these integrations can handle everything from lead generation to final sale reconciliation, creating a harmonious, automated ecosystem.

Furthermore, leveraging cloud technology can streamline your operations significantly. Services like Amazon Web Services (AWS), Microsoft Azure, or Google Cloud provide scalable storage and computing power, enabling you to manage and process data without investing in expensive hardware. The cloud also facilitates remote work, allowing your team to collaborate in real-time from anywhere in the world.

It's also worth mentioning the increasing role of the Internet of Things (IoT) in business automation. IoT devices can monitor and control various aspects of your operations, from climate control in your warehouse to predictive maintenance of machinery. This level of automation reduces downtime and operational costs, ensuring your business runs smoothly.

Don't overlook the value of automation in human resources (HR) either. Tools like BambooHR or Workday handle everything from recruitment to employee performance tracking, automating repetitive HR tasks and allowing your team to focus on strategic initiatives. Automated onboarding processes ensure that new hires are brought up to speed efficiently, contributing to a smoother operation.

As you integrate more technology into your business, remember the importance of scalability. Choose tools that can grow with your business, offering more advanced features as your needs evolve. This flexibility ensures that your investment in technology continues to deliver value, supporting your business's growth journey.

It's also essential to keep an eye on emerging technologies. Innovations like blockchain, augmented reality (AR), and virtual reality (VR) are starting to make significant impacts in various industries. Staying informed and prepared to leverage these technologies can provide a competitive edge, opening new avenues for automation and efficiency.

Finally, fostering a culture that embraces technology is key. Invest in training your team to understand and utilize these tools effectively. Encourage them to explore new technologies and experiment with automation in their workflows. A tech-savvy team is essential for fully leveraging the benefits of automation, driving your business towards continuous improvement and growth.

In summary, leveraging technology in automating your business isn't just about adopting the latest trends. It's about carefully selecting and integrating tools that address your unique challenges, streamline operations, and scale your efforts. By doing so, you free up valuable time and resources, allowing you to focus on innovating and growing your business. So, dive into the world of technology, automate those repetitive tasks, and watch as your business transforms and thrives.

Outsourcing Tasks

When it comes to automating your business, one of the most effective strategies you'll encounter is outsourcing tasks. As an entrepreneur with aspirations of reaching your first $1 million, understanding the nuances of outsourcing can be a game-changer. But let's be real, delegating parts of your business to others can be both exhilarating and daunting. It's all about finding the right balance.

First off, let's dispel a common myth: outsourcing isn't about offloading the tasks you don't want to do—it's about elevating your business by leveraging expertise that you may not possess. Picture this: you're fantastic at developing products but terrible at customer service. By outsourcing your customer support, you're not shirking your responsibilities; you're ensuring that your customers get the best experience possible. And happy customers are returning customers.

Now, where do you start? It can be overwhelming given the sheer number of platforms and services available today. To make it simpler, start by identifying repetitive tasks that consume a lot of your time and don't directly contribute to business growth. Bookkeeping, data entry, and even certain aspects of marketing are prime candidates. Think of it like this: if a task can be documented and taught, it can be outsourced.

Consider platforms like Upwork, Fiverr, and Freelancer. These platforms have granular rating systems and reviews, which make it easier to find qualified professionals. Another option is specialized agencies, particularly for more complex tasks like digital marketing or software development. They bring a level of credibility and reliability that individual freelancers may not offer.

You'll also need to think about cost. Outsourcing can be a money-saver, but it's crucial to approach it with a cost-benefit analysis mindset. Rather than focusing purely on the price tag, weigh the value you're getting against the cost. For instance, hiring a seasoned graphic designer might be pricier upfront, but the professional branding will pay dividends down the road in customer perception and engagement.

On the flip side, don't fall into the trap of micromanaging. Trust is a significant factor when you outsource. You've vetted these professionals for a reason, so give them the space to do what they do best. Set clear expectations and deadlines but avoid hovering over every minor detail. Micromanagement defeats the purpose of outsourcing and, frankly, wastes your time, which defeats the objective of automation entirely.

Communication is the backbone of successful outsourcing. Regular check-ins and updates create a seamless flow of work. Utilize tools such as Asana, Slack, or Trello to keep everyone on the same page. These communications platforms streamline activities, making it easy to see who's working on what and ensuring tasks are completed on time.

Don't forget about quality assurance. Even when you outsource tasks, the final responsibility rests with you. Implement a review process to ensure everything meets your standards. Whether it's a marketing campaign, a software module, or customer service responses, review the output and provide constructive feedback. This not only maintains high standards but also fosters a collaborative relationship with your outsourced team.

There's a strategic element to outsourcing that often gets overlooked: scaling. As your business grows, the demand on your time and resources will multiply. Initially, you might start with one or two freelancers. However, as your needs expand, you might consider building an entire remote team. You can create a hybrid work environment where essential functions are managed in-house, while other tasks are outsourced.

CHAPTER 14: AUTOMATING YOUR BUSINESS

Have you heard about Virtual Assistants (VAs)? These are versatile professionals who can handle a myriad of tasks from scheduling meetings to managing emails, allowing you to focus on high-level activities. For many entrepreneurs, VAs are the secret sauce to a streamlined and efficient operation. Platforms such as Zirtual and Belay are excellent starting points to find qualified VAs.

One thing that can't be stressed enough is the importance of documenting your processes before you begin outsourcing. Creating a comprehensive Standard Operating Procedure (SOP) for each task ensures consistency and quality. It might seem tedious at first, but this step is invaluable for smooth transitions and maintaining high standards of work.

Security is another critical aspect. When outsourcing, you're often sharing confidential information and access to various systems. Ensure you use secure platforms and agreements that protect your data. Non-Disclosure Agreements (NDAs) can add an extra layer of security. Platforms like LastPass make sharing passwords secure and straightforward without exposing sensitive information.

To sum it up, outsourcing tasks is a proactive strategy to free up your time, tap into specialized skills, and scale your business in a sustainable way. It's not just about reducing workload; it's about being strategic in optimizing your operations. By delegating effectively, you're buying back your most valuable commodity: time. Time to innovate, strategize, and propel your business towards that $1 million mark.

Take it from successful entrepreneurs: they didn't go at it alone. They built networks of highly skilled professionals who could execute their vision. Your journey to $1 million won't be an isolated effort. Outsourcing is your first step in building a collaborative, efficient, and scalable business machine.

So, as you work through your one-year plan, remember: every minute you save by outsourcing is a minute you can spend on what truly matters—growing your business and achieving your dreams. Automate smartly, outsource effectively, and watch your business soar.

Chapter 15: Advanced Marketing Strategies

Welcome to the stage where marketing innovatively takes center stage. This chapter is all about pushing the envelope with your marketing efforts to propel your business closer to that million-dollar mark. Advanced marketing is about layering sophistication onto your existing strategies. If you've mastered the basics, it's time to dive into the power of email marketing and the richness of content marketing. These aren't just buzzwords – they're tools that drive engagement and build a loyal customer base. Think of email marketing as your direct line to customers' inboxes, where you can share offers, updates, and personalized content that clicks. Content marketing, on the other hand, is your playground to showcase expertise through blogs, videos, and social media posts. Don't just aim to sell; aim to educate, entertain, and inspire. These advanced tactics require a blend of creativity and data analysis, harnessing the full potential of modern tools to measure, tweak, and perfect your approach. It's time to channel your inner marketing auteur and create a strategy that's as dynamic and ambitious as your business.

Email Marketing

Email marketing isn't just another tool in your marketing arsenal; it's a juggernaut when used effectively. Think of it as a direct line to your audience's attention spans, wallets, and, ultimately, their hearts. It's cost-effective, personalized, and measurable. It's your opportunity to build relationships at scale, make announcements with precision, and drive sales with compelling calls-to-action. Whether you're an entrepreneur, a budding business owner, or just someone with a passion project, email marketing can be a game-changer in your journey to your first $1 million.

First things first, let's talk about the basics. You need an email list. This isn't something you can just buy off the internet and call it a day. Building an organic, engaged email list is essential. Quality trumps quantity every single time in email marketing. Start by capturing emails from your website visitors, social media followers, or even from in-person events. Utilize lead magnets like free e-books, special discounts, or exclusive content to entice people to subscribe. The goal is to provide value upfront, so they're excited to hear from you.

Once you've built your email list, the next step is segmenting it. Not everyone in your audience wants the same thing. Some might be interested in new product launches, while others might love behind-the-scenes stories and tips. By segmenting your list, you can send more relevant content to your subscribers, which in turn increases open rates, click-through rates, and, ultimately, conversions. Use data to drive these decisions. Look at purchase history, browsing behavior, and even demographic information to personalize the experience as much as possible.

Speaking of content, what should you be sending these people? The possibilities are endless, but the core idea is to add value. This could be educational content that solves a problem your audience faces, promotional content with special offers, or even entertaining content that aligns with your brand's voice. The key is to mix it up and keep it fresh. Nobody wants to receive the same kind of email over and over again. Test different formats and measure the results. See what resonates and double down on that.

Then comes the magic of crafting the perfect email. Pay attention to the subject line – it's your first impression, and you don't get a second chance to make a first impression. Make it intriguing, yet clear. Avoid spammy words and excessive punctuation, as these can trigger spam filters. Next, focus on the email body. Keep it concise and scannable. Use subheadings, bullet points, and imagery to break up the text. Have a clear call to action (CTA). Whether it's "Shop Now," "Read More," or "Download," make sure your CTA stands out and tells the subscriber exactly what you want them to do.

When it comes to frequency, find a balance that works for you and your audience. Too frequent, and you'll end up in the spam folder; too sparse, and you'll be forgotten. Start with a consistent schedule, like weekly or bi-weekly emails. Monitor your email metrics to adjust frequency. If you notice higher unsubscribe rates or lower open rates, you might be emailing too often.

Metrics are your best friend in email marketing. Analyzing your email campaigns will give you insights into what's working and what's not. Look at metrics like open rates, click-through rates, conversion rates, and unsubscribe rates. Use A/B testing to experiment with different subject lines, email copy, images, and CTAs. The data you collect will help you refine your strategy and maximize your return on investment (ROI).

Automation is another crucial aspect of an effective email marketing strategy. Automation tools can help you send the right message at the right time. For example, you can set up a welcome email series for new subscribers, abandoned cart reminders for those who didn't complete a purchase, or re-engagement campaigns for subscribers who have gone silent. Automation not only saves you time but also ensures you're nurturing relationships consistently.

One thing to remember is to always comply with email marketing laws and regulations, like the CAN-SPAM Act in the United States. Always include a way for subscribers to opt-out, and make sure your subject lines and email content are not misleading. Respecting your subscribers' privacy and preferences builds trust and long-term loyalty.

Lastly, always be testing and evolving your email marketing strategy. The digital landscape is ever-changing, and staying ahead means continuously learning and adapting. Subscribe to industry newsletters, attend webinars, and follow thought leaders to keep your strategy fresh and effective. Your email marketing efforts should evolve as your business grows and as you gain more insights into what your subscribers love and expect from you.

In conclusion, email marketing is a robust, adaptable, and high-return strategy that deserves your focus. From building an engaged list to sending targeted, valuable content, to analyzing metrics and automating campaigns, each step compounds in value. Mastering email marketing can significantly accelerate your path to achieving $1 million and beyond. So, roll up your sleeves, dive into the data, and start crafting emails that deliver substantial results.

Content Marketing

Have you ever thought about how some companies manage to stay constantly on top of the minds of their customers? That's right, it's no accident. They're using content marketing. This powerful strategy goes beyond the straightforward push of traditional advertising, focusing on providing valuable, relevant content that speaks directly to the needs and interests of your audience.

Let's be real - content marketing isn't just about writing blog posts or churning out social media updates. It's about creating a holistic, multi-channel experience that guides your potential customers through every stage of their buying journey. If executed correctly, it can turn casual surfers into loyal brand advocates. How do you do this? By consistently delivering value, building trust, and encouraging engagement.

First off, the key to a successful content marketing plan starts with understanding your audience. Conducting market research to identify their pain points, interests, and behaviors will help you tailor your content to meet their specific needs. Knowing what makes them tick allows you to craft messages that resonate deeply and prompt action.

Once you understand your audience, it's time to develop a content strategy. This involves setting clear objectives about what you want to achieve with your content. Do you want to drive more traffic to your website, increase brand awareness, or boost sales? Your goals will dictate the type of content you create and the platforms you use to distribute it.

Content pillars are another crucial element. These are the main themes or categories your content will revolve around. For instance, if you're in the fitness industry, your pillars might include workout tips, healthy recipes, and mental wellness. Having defined pillars ensures that your content remains focused and relevant to your audience.

Now that you've got your strategy and pillars in place, let's talk about *content formats*. Diversifying your content types can help you reach a wider audience and keep your existing followers engaged. Blog posts are great for detailed information, but don't overlook the power of videos, infographics, podcasts, and even memes. Each format has its unique advantages and can cater to different segments of your audience.

One of the biggest game changers in content marketing is the art of storytelling. People are hardwired to respond to stories, making it an effective way to connect on an emotional level. Whether you're sharing customer success stories, behind-the-scenes looks at your business, or your personal entrepreneurial journey, storytelling can make your content more relatable and engaging.

Distribution is equally important as creation. Simply producing content isn't enough if it's not reaching your target audience. Invest time in promoting your content through various channels. Social media, email newsletters, and guest posts on relevant websites are all effective ways to broaden your content's reach. Consider using paid promotion techniques like sponsored posts or targeted ads to further amplify your message.

SEO, or search engine optimization, should not be overlooked. This involves optimizing your content to rank higher in search engine results, making it easier for potential customers to find you. Using the right keywords, creating high-quality content, and earning backlinks from reputable sites are all part of an effective SEO strategy. Think of SEO as a long-term investment that pays off by driving organic traffic to your website.

Content marketing is also about consistency. Posting sporadically won't yield the desired results. Develop a content calendar to plan and schedule your posts ahead of time. This helps you maintain a regular posting frequency, keeps your audience engaged, and ensures you're covering all your content pillars adequately.

Metrics and analytics are your best friends. Tracking the performance of your content is crucial for understanding what works and what doesn't. Use tools like Google Analytics, social media insights, and email marketing reports to measure engagement, track conversions, and identify areas for improvement. Continuously analyzing these metrics allows you to refine your strategy and maximize your return on investment.

Let's not forget the importance of **repurposing content**. One piece of content can be transformed into multiple formats to reach different audiences. For instance, a well-researched blog post can be broken down into smaller social media posts, converted into a video script, or even discussed in a podcast. This not only extends the life of your content but also maximizes your efforts.

User-generated content is another powerful tool at your disposal. Encouraging your audience to create content related to your brand can significantly boost your marketing efforts. Think of testimonials, reviews, photos, or videos of customers using your product. Showcasing this content on your platforms builds trust and authenticity.

Involving different members of your team in content creation can bring diverse perspectives and skillsets into the mix. This not only helps in generating fresh, varied content but also fosters a sense of ownership and collaboration within your team. Whether it's your product designer writing a blog post about the design process or your customer service rep sharing common customer queries, each team member can add unique value.

Building a community around your content can exponentially enhance its impact. Engage with your audience by responding to comments, hosting live sessions, and creating interactive content like polls or quizzes. A strong community fosters loyalty and encourages organic sharing, further expanding your reach.

Don't be afraid to innovate and experiment. The digital landscape is continuously evolving, and what works today might not work tomorrow. Keep an eye on emerging trends and be willing to try new formats or platforms. Whether it's launching a podcast, creating a virtual reality experience, or exploring TikTok, staying ahead of the curve can give you a competitive edge.

Finally, understand that content marketing is a long-term game. It takes time to see tangible results, so patience and persistence are key. Stay committed to delivering value, continue refining your strategy based on data and feedback, and most importantly, remain genuine in your efforts. Content marketing isn't just about making sales—it's about building relationships and trust that will pay dividends in the long run.

Remember, content marketing isn't just a tactic, it's a fundamental aspect of modern business strategy. And as you embark on this journey, you'll find that the true power of content marketing lies in its ability to connect, engage, and inspire at a deeper level. With the right approach, you're not just marketing a product; you're building a brand and creating lasting relationships with your audience.

Chapter 16: Building a Brand

Building a brand is about more than just a cool logo or a catchy slogan. It's about crafting a story that resonates, staying consistent in your messaging across all platforms, and creating an emotional connection with your audience. Think of it as the soul of your business; it's what makes people choose you over competitors time and time again. Start by defining your brand story, which should stem from your core values and mission. Then, ensure every piece of content, product, and customer interaction aligns with that story. Authenticity is key, so don't be afraid to share your journey, your struggles, and your triumphs. By doing so, you'll create a reliable and relatable brand that people not only trust but advocate for. The relationships you build will become the foundation of your long-term success, ultimately guiding you to that coveted first million and beyond.

Crafting Your Brand Story

Your brand story isn't just something you write up in a marketing meeting; it's the narrative that will encapsulate the essence of your business. It serves to connect you with your customers on a deeper emotional level. A well-crafted brand story is instrumental in distinguishing you from the competition. Even more, it can ignite passion, loyalty, and trust among your audience. But how do you go about crafting a compelling brand story? Let's dive into the key components and process.

First and foremost, your brand story begins with "why." Why did you start this venture? What problem are you solving? Establishing a strong "why" can provide a solid foundation that resonates with people. Entrepreneurs often kick off their businesses for personal reasons or because they've identified a gap in the market that they're passionate about filling. Your "why" is the bedrock of your brand story and should be consistent in every piece of content you create.

Next, consider the hero of your story. Contrary to what you might think, the hero isn't you or your business; it's your customer. Your brand exists to serve your customers and improve their lives in some way. By positioning your customers as the heroes, you make your brand story more relatable and compelling.

Let's talk about the villain. In every story, there's a challenge or a problem that the hero must overcome. In your brand narrative, this challenge could be anything—from inefficient solutions offered by other businesses to everyday frustrations your customers face. Clearly defining the problem helps your audience see the value in your brand as the solution.

Your brand's values and mission also play a significant role in crafting your story. Values are the principles that guide your business decisions; they're the moral compass that steers your brand. Your mission is the big-picture goal you aim to accomplish. Both elements should be ingrained in your brand story, providing a consistent theme that runs through all your messaging.

Don't forget to add a personal touch to your brand story. Authenticity is key. Share anecdotes, personal challenges, and triumphs that illustrate your journey. People connect with other people, not faceless corporations. By opening up about your experiences, you can establish a more human connection with your audience.

Visual storytelling is another crucial component. Images, videos, and even the design elements of your brand can communicate aspects of your story without words. Consistency in visual elements like your logo, color palette, and typography reinforces your brand identity.

As you craft your story, remember to keep it simple and focused. A convoluted or overly complex narrative can confuse your audience and muddy your message. Stick to the core elements that define your brand and build on them.

CHAPTER 16: BUILDING A BRAND

Once you have a draft of your story, test it out with a few trusted advisors or even some loyal customers. Get their feedback and make adjustments as necessary. Does it resonate with them? Are there parts that seem unclear or unconvincing? Use their inputs to refine and polish your brand narrative.

Your brand story should be not only clear and cohesive but also adaptable. As your business grows and evolves, so too may your story. Be open to tweaking it to reflect new directions, innovations, and achievements. Keeping your story relevant will ensure it continues to resonate with your audience.

Now, where do you share this brand story? Everywhere. It should be evident on your website's About page, present in your social media profiles, and woven into your customer service interactions. Every piece of marketing material you produce should reflect elements of your brand story so that it becomes ingrained in the public's perception of who you are and what you stand for.

As an entrepreneur, your time is often split between various activities, from developing products to managing operations. But investing time in crafting and refining your brand story can yield dividends far beyond the initial effort. It turns casual customers into loyal advocates, enhances your marketing campaigns, and builds an emotional connection that competitors will find hard to break.

In conclusion, crafting your brand story is not just an exercise in creative writing; it's a strategic tool that lays the foundation of your brand's relationship with customers. It requires introspection about your "why," understanding your customers' needs, clearly defining the problem you solve, and infusing your values and personal touch. Make it visually appealing, test it, refine it, and make sure it permeates every aspect of your brand's presence. Do this well, and you'll create a narrative that not only stands out but sticks with your audience for the long haul.

Your brand story is the heart and soul of your business. It's what makes you unique and memorable in a crowded marketplace. So, get started on your narrative today, and watch as it transforms not just your marketing efforts but the very way your customers perceive and interact with your brand.

Consistent Brand Messaging

At the core of building a brand lies the art of communicating your message consistently. This is not just about having a flashy slogan or a neat logo—though those help—but about creating a cohesive narrative that permeates every interaction your customers have with your business. This consistency fosters trust, recognition, and loyalty, essential ingredients for reaching that $1 million milestone.

First off, let's talk about why consistent brand messaging is non-negotiable. Think about some of the world's most recognizable brands. What do they all have in common? Whether it's the golden arches of McDonald's or the sleek apple of, well, Apple, these brands exude a uniform message across all platforms. This reliability tells their audience that they are dependable and trustworthy. If your messaging is all over the place, it won't be long before potential customers start to feel confused or misled. Confusion is a brand killer.

So, how do you ensure consistency? Begin with your brand's core values and mission. These should serve as the foundation for all your messaging efforts. Every piece of content, every advertisement, every social media post should echo these fundamental principles. For instance, if your brand stands for sustainability, any deviation from that message can dilute your brand's identity. Imagine if Patagonia, known for its environmental stance, suddenly began promoting fast fashion—customers would feel betrayed, and the brand's credibility would take a hit.

In practical terms, consistency involves standardizing your brand's voice and visual elements. Your brand voice—the tone and style in which you communicate—should be uniform across all touchpoints. If your brand is casual and friendly, like Wendy's social media presence, maintain that tone even in more formal contexts like press releases. This doesn't mean you cannot adapt slightly based on the audience, but the core elements should stay the same.

Visual consistency is equally important. This includes your color scheme, typography, and logo usage. Creating a style guide can be immensely helpful.

A style guide is a document that outlines how every element of your brand should look and feel. This should be shared with everyone in your company to ensure all outward-facing communication aligns with your brand's identity.

But what about when your business evolves? Great question. Brands often need to adapt and refresh to stay relevant. When undergoing such changes, the key is to reintroduce your brand thoughtfully. Communicate the updates clearly to your audience, explaining why changes are being made and how they benefit them. Take the example of Old Spice, which successfully reinvented itself to appeal to a younger audience while maintaining core elements recognizable to its existing customer base. The key takeaway? Evolution doesn't mean you abandon your principles; it means you realign them with current market needs without confusing your audience.

Consistency extends to customer service as well. How your team handles inquiries, complaints, and feedback says volumes about your brand. A scripted and uniform approach ensures that every customer interaction reflects your brand values. For example, Zappos is famous for its exceptional customer service, which consistently aligns with its brand message of delivering happiness.

Also, consider the channels through which you communicate. Your website, social media, emails, and even physical stores (if you have them) should all provide a seamless experience. Inconsistent experiences across these platforms can create friction and reduce trust. Each channel should feel like a different room in the same house, not a completely separate entity.

Another vital aspect is your storytelling. Your brand story should be told consistently across all platforms and touchpoints. This narrative is more than just a history lesson; it's about expressing why you do what you do in a way that resonates with your target audience. When told right, this story becomes a powerful tool for forging emotional connections and fostering loyalty.

To keep your brand messaging aligned internally, regular training and updates are necessary. Conduct workshops and create resources for your team to ensure everyone is on the same page. Remember, every person in your organization is a brand ambassador, whether they are in the marketing department or on the production floor.

Don't forget about your partners and collaborators. Whether it's influencers, affiliates, or service providers, anyone who represents your brand should understand and follow your brand guidelines. Clear communication and contracts can help ensure that everyone is working towards the same goal and delivering a uniform message.

Metrics and feedback also play a crucial role. Regularly measure the effectiveness of your brand messaging and be open to feedback. Use surveys, social listening tools, and performance analytics to gauge how well your message is being received and where improvements can be made. An iterative process of refinement and adjustment will help keep your brand aligned with its core values while remaining relevant to your audience.

In conclusion, consistent brand messaging is not a one-and-done task but an ongoing commitment. It requires careful planning, monitoring, and adjustment to ensure that your brand's identity shines through every piece of communication. By maintaining a cohesive message, not only will you cultivate a loyal customer base, but you'll also forge a strong, recognizable brand that stands the test of time.

So as you forge ahead in your entrepreneurial journey, remember: consistency is king. Your brand is a promise to your customers, and every facet of your business should work towards keeping that promise. The pathway to your first $1 million will be paved with challenges and opportunities, and a consistent brand message will be your guiding star, ensuring that you not only reach your destination but thrive long after.

Chapter 17: Analyzing Metrics

Here's where the magic of your hard work starts to reveal itself—analyzing metrics is like having a roadmap to your million-dollar goal. You're going to dive deep into Key Performance Indicators (KPIs) and harness the power of data to drive your decisions. Now, don't get bogged down in numbers; rather, see them as insights that light the path forward. Track what's working and what's not, refine your strategies, and pivot when necessary. Make it a habit to measure everything from conversion rates to customer acquisition costs. This data-driven approach empowers you to tweak, adapt, and grow with confidence, ensuring every move you make is a step closer to that seven-figure milestone.

Key Performance Indicators (KPIs)

Key Performance Indicators, or KPIs, are essentially the heartbeat of your business. Think of KPIs as the metrics that provide insight into the health and performance of your venture. They are not just numbers on a spreadsheet; they embody the progress and success of your business, guiding you toward your million-dollar goal.

Let's start with the basics. KPIs are specific, measurable values that help you understand how effectively you are achieving your business objectives. Every business has different KPIs depending on its goals, industry, and operational format. For example, an e-commerce store might prioritize conversion rates and average order values, while a subscription-based service might focus on customer retention and churn rate. The magic of KPIs lies in their ability to distill complex data into easily understandable indicators of success.

You can't improve what you don't measure. This principle is why KPIs are indispensable. They help you identify areas of strength and pinpoint where there's room for improvement. Think of KPIs as your business' personal trainer, continually pushing you toward peak performance. They ensure that your decisions are data-driven, bolstering your strategies with the rigors of quantitative analysis.

In the early stages, your KPIs might focus heavily on customer acquisition, conversion rates, and revenue growth. Months 0-4 are all about finding your niche, understanding your customer, and generating those all-important initial sales. One critical KPI during this period is the Customer Acquisition Cost (CAC). This metric helps you understand how much you're spending to acquire each new customer—an essential figure to keep track of as you allocate your budget and refine your marketing strategies.

Moving into the growth phase, KPIs should evolve to include metrics related to scalability and efficiency. For instance, Months 5-8 might emphasize Cost Per Click (CPC) if you're running advertising campaigns, and Customer Lifetime Value (CLV) to gauge the long-term profitability of each client. These KPIs take into account not just immediate returns but the overall efficiency and future revenue potential of your efforts.

Never underestimate the power of retention metrics. As you progress to late-stage growth (Months 9-12), customer retention becomes a significant focus. High Churn Rates can eat away at your profits, making it much harder to reach your goals. Tracking Net Promoter Score (NPS) can provide insight into customer satisfaction and loyalty, giving you actionable data to improve customer experience and foster long-term relationships.

Financial KPIs such as Gross Profit Margin and Net Profit Margin should always be on your radar. These metrics will give you a clear understanding of how much profit you are making after accounting for all costs. In the drive towards your first million, optimizing these financial indicators can spell the difference between success and failure.

Inventory management metrics, such as Inventory Turnover Ratio and Stock Out Rate, also play a crucial role, particularly in product-based businesses. Efficient inventory management can lower costs and increase profitability, keeping cash flow smooth and operations humming.

Keeping track of your KPIs can be overwhelming, but the right tools can simplify this process. Various software solutions offer dashboards to visualize your KPIs in real-time, making it easier to react swiftly to new data. Automation tools that integrate with your existing systems can also collect data seamlessly, allowing you to focus on interpreting and acting on the insights.

While KPIs provide a snapshot of your business health, remember that context is key. Benchmarking your KPIs against industry standards or competitors can offer valuable insights. This comparative analysis can highlight areas where you are excelling and where you need to catch up.

Don't set and forget your KPIs. Regularly review and adjust them as your business evolves. What's relevant in the initial months might shift as you grow and expand. Create a feedback loop where KPIs not only measure success but also inform and shape your strategy moving forward.

Finally, KPIs aren't just for the leadership team; they're for everyone. Communicating your KPIs transparently with your team can foster a culture of shared goals and collective effort. Make these metrics a part of team meetings, and celebrate the milestones reached. The motivation derived from hitting a KPI can be a powerful driver for sustained performance.

To sum up, KPIs are more than just metrics—they are strategic tools that guide your journey towards business success. Understanding and monitoring them can help you make informed decisions, optimize your operations, and ultimately achieve your goal of hitting your first $1 million. Stay focused, stay informed, and let your KPIs light the way.

Data-Driven Decisions

In the business world, decisions grounded in data can be the difference between thriving and barely surviving. Analyzing metrics isn't just a tedious task; it's the lifeline of a growing business. Whether you're an entrepreneur, a student, or a parent venturing into the business landscape, using data effectively can propel you toward your goal of hitting that first $1 million.

So, let's start with the basics: What does it mean to make data-driven decisions? At its core, it's about letting empirical evidence guide your actions. Data takes the guesswork out of the equation and gives you tangible insights into what's working and what's not. It's like having a cheat sheet in an exam but totally legit and highly recommended.

Imagine you're running an online store. You need to know how many people visit your site, what they click on, and at what point they abandon their cart. These metrics can be eye-opening. They tell you where you're losing potential customers and where you could be turning casual browsers into buyers. Taking action based on this data can dramatically improve your conversion rates.

You'll find all kinds of data tools out there—Google Analytics, customer relationship management (CRM) systems, and even custom dashboards tailored to your business needs. Embrace these tools like a kid in a candy store. The more you utilize them, the clearer the picture of your business health becomes.

Data-driven decisions go beyond just tracking website traffic or sales numbers. For example, you might notice a pattern that customers often purchase a particular product alongside another item. In this case, you could bundle these items together for a combo deal, increasing your average order value and boosting sales.

However, not all data is useful data. You need to distinguish between noise and meaningful information. Focus on Key Performance Indicators (KPIs) that directly impact your bottom line. Monthly recurring revenue, customer acquisition cost, and customer lifetime value are among the critical KPIs you should monitor. Paying attention to the right metrics helps you make informed decisions without getting bogged down by irrelevant details.

The next step is to continuously test and iterate based on the data. Maybe you've launched a marketing campaign that isn't performing as expected. Rather than scrapping it altogether, analyze why it's not yielding results. Is the messaging off? Are you targeting the wrong audience? Use the data to tweak your approach and run A/B tests to compare different strategies.

Through a process of refinement, your campaigns will become more effective over time.

Now, let's talk about predictive analytics. This involves using historical data to forecast future trends. For instance, if you see a consistent spike in sales every December, you can prepare for this season by stocking up on inventory and ramping up your marketing efforts ahead of time. Predictive analytics turns past data into a crystal ball, giving you a clearer view of future possibilities.

But don't just collect data for the sake of it. Everyone on your team should understand how to interpret the numbers and what actions to take based on them. Create a culture where data-sharing is second nature. Encourage your team to use data in their day-to-day decision-making process, from marketing to product development to customer service.

Remember, data is not just about numbers on a spreadsheet. It's about people—your customers. Use customer feedback and reviews as qualitative data to compliment the quantitative metrics. Sometimes, a few poignant comments from customers can offer insights that numbers fail to reveal. Combining both types of data provides a more holistic view of your business landscape.

A practical tip for incorporating data into your decisions is setting up automated reports. Many analytics tools allow you to schedule regular reports to be sent directly to your inbox. This keeps vital metrics at your fingertips without having to dig for them. Automation saves time and ensures you never miss a critical insight.

Finally, don't shy away from external data sources. Market trends, competitor analysis, and industry benchmarks provide context to your internal metrics. Understanding where you stand in the larger ecosystem can help you set realistic targets and strategies to achieve them.

Embrace the world of data as a continuous, evolving journey. The landscape changes quickly, new tools emerge, and market dynamics shift. Stay curious and adaptable, always seeking to refine your approach based on the latest data available.

Data-driven decisions aren't just for big corporations. Small businesses, startups, and even solo entrepreneurs can harness the power of data. The barriers to entry are lower than ever, and the potential benefits are enormous. When you get it right, data becomes a powerful ally in achieving your first $1 million and beyond.

So go ahead, dive into your metrics, let the data guide your next big decision, and watch your business soar.

Chapter 18: Optimizing Profit Margins

When it comes to optimizing profit margins, think of it as the art of balancing elements that boost revenue while tightening the belt on expenses. You've got to scrutinize every aspect of your operations to uncover where you can cut costs without compromising quality or customer satisfaction. Focus on cost-effective sourcing, negotiate better terms with suppliers, and always be on the lookout for waste. On the flip side, increasing your average order value can skyrocket your margins. Offer bundles, upsell complementary products, or introduce loyalty programs that encourage repeat business. By keeping a sharp eye on both sides of the equation, you'll craft a lean operation that maximizes every dollar earned, paving the way to your first million with greater efficiency and confidence. It's not just about making more; it's about keeping more.

Cost Reduction Strategies

When we talk about optimizing profit margins, one of the most effective strategies is identifying and implementing cost reduction strategies. In essence, the less you spend to operate your business, the more you can retain as profit. Of course, this doesn't mean compromising on quality or cutting corners. Rather, it's about being smart and strategic, finding areas where you can trim the fat without weakening your business.

First, let's talk about inventory management. Holding excess inventory ties up capital and storage costs. By adopting just-in-time inventory practices, you can reduce the amount of stock you need to keep on hand. This means working closely with suppliers to ensure timely deliveries and using inventory management software that helps track and predict inventory needs accurately. Efficient inventory management can significantly reduce waste and associated costs.

Now, let's discuss outsourcing. Hiring full-time employees can be costly, considering salaries, benefits, and taxes. Outsourcing certain tasks to freelancers or agencies can be a more cost-effective solution. This is particularly useful for specialized tasks like graphic design, content creation, or even certain administrative tasks. You only pay for what you need when you need it, without the overhead costs associated with full-time employees.

Another powerful strategy is negotiating with suppliers. Building robust relationships with your suppliers can give you leverage to negotiate better terms. Don't hesitate to ask for discounts, bulk deals, or extended payment terms. Sometimes, it's just a matter of asking. You'd be surprised how often suppliers are willing to work with you, especially if you're a loyal customer.

Energy efficiency is another area where you can save. Implementing energy-saving practices, like switching to LED lighting, using energy-efficient equipment, and optimizing heating/cooling systems, can significantly reduce your utility bills. These savings may seem small on a daily basis but can add up to a considerable amount over the year.

Look into automating repetitive tasks. Automation tools can handle tasks like email marketing, social media posts, bookkeeping, and customer relationship management (CRM). While there might be an upfront cost, over time, automation can save you a significant amount of money by reducing the hours spent on these manual tasks and improving efficiency.

Don't underestimate the power of going digital. Digital products and services often have lower overhead than their physical counterparts. Consider shifting more of your offerings to digital formats if applicable. This can reduce production, shipping, and storage costs. Even something simple like offering digital receipts instead of printed ones can reduce costs and environmental impact.

A subscription model can also be a clever cost reduction strategy. Offering your products or services on a subscription basis can ensure steady, predictable revenue and reduce marketing costs associated with acquiring new customers. It's often easier and cheaper to retain existing customers than to find new ones.

Leverage shared economy platforms. Instead of purchasing expensive equipment or office space, consider leasing or using co-working spaces and shared equipment. This is particularly useful for startups or small businesses that don't need their own high-end facilities or equipment all the time.

Don't forget about tax strategies. Ensure you're taking full advantage of all tax deductions and credits available to your business. Consult with a tax professional who can help identify areas where you can save. Sometimes, small changes in how you structure your finances can lead to significant tax savings.

Looking at your marketing spend, it's essential to be as targeted and efficient as possible. Data-driven marketing helps you get the most return on your investment. Use analytics to track which strategies are working and which aren't. Cut out the non-performing channels and double down on what's actually driving sales.

Outdated technology can also be a drain on your resources. Upgrading to more efficient systems or software can lead to considerable cost savings through increased productivity and lower maintenance costs. Sometimes, the most cost-effective solution is to invest in better tools upfront.

Evaluate your recurring expenses regularly. Service providers often raise their rates over time, banking on your inertia. Periodically reviewing services like phone, internet, and insurance and shopping around for better deals can lead to substantial savings without sacrificing quality.

Lastly, embrace a culture of cost-consciousness within your team. Train your employees to think like owners and be mindful of costs. Simple actions like turning off lights when not in use, using materials efficiently, and suggesting cost-saving ideas can collectively lead to substantial savings.

Implementing these cost reduction strategies requires both strategic thinking and a bit of creativity. The goal is not just to cut costs but to do so in a way that supports long-term growth and sustainability. The investment you make in smart, innovative cost reductions today can pave the way for a more profitable and resilient business in the future. Remember, every dollar saved is a dollar that contributes directly to your bottom line. So, let's identify those opportunities, act on them, and optimize those profit margins like a pro. Keep pushing, keep improving, and keep your eyes on that million-dollar milestone.

Increasing Average Order Value

So, you're ready to dive into the world of maximizing your profit margins. One of the most effective ways to do this is by increasing your average order value (AOV). The higher the AOV, the more revenue you can generate from each customer, all while spending the same amount on customer acquisition. It's like getting a higher return on investment without having to reinvent the wheel every time.

First things first, let's break down what average order value actually means. Put simply, AOV is the average amount of money each customer spends per transaction. It's calculated by dividing your total revenue by the number of orders. Simple, right? But the strategies to increase it can be varied and nuanced.

One classic method to boost AOV is upselling and cross-selling. Upselling involves encouraging customers to purchase a higher-end version of the product they're interested in. For example, if someone's buying a laptop, you might show them a more powerful version with added features. Cross-selling, on the other hand, involves suggesting complementary products. If someone's buying running shoes, you could recommend running socks or a water bottle. These techniques work because they cater to the customer's purchase intent and add value to their original choice.

Another powerful strategy is bundling products. Bundles create a perception of value by offering a discount when multiple items are bought together. Take, for instance, the classic fast-food meal deal: a burger, fries, and a drink. Buying these together usually costs less than buying them separately. Not only does this increase the AOV, but it also helps in clearing out inventory faster and enticing customers to try new products.

Let's not forget the magic of limited-time offers and discounts. Flash sales, seasonal discounts, and exclusive promotions can drive urgency and boost the AOV. However, it's crucial to balance this with maintaining your profit margins. The trick is to structure these promotions in a way that increases overall spend without significantly eating into your costs. For instance, "spend $100 and get 15% off" can effectively nudge customers to add more items to their cart to reach that threshold.

Personalization plays a key role in increasing AOV. With advances in AI and machine learning, businesses can now offer tailored recommendations based on individual browsing and purchase history. Think of Amazon's "customers who bought this also bought" section. This type of customization creates a more engaging shopping experience and encourages customers to purchase additional products.

Loyalty programs can also be incredibly effective. By rewarding repeat purchases or higher spending, you can incentivize customers to buy more. Points systems, tiered memberships, and exclusive member discounts create a sense of community and loyalty. For example, a coffee shop offering a free drink after every ten purchases not only encourages frequent visits but might also inspire customers to spend a little more each time to get to that freebie faster.

Another approach is to optimize your pricing strategy. Psychological pricing, for example, can make a significant difference. Pricing something at $9.99 instead of $10.00 can psychologically appear cheaper and more attractive to customers, even if the difference is just a cent. Similarly, introducing decoy pricing—where a middle option makes the higher-priced one seem like a better deal—can nudge customers towards more expensive products.

Free shipping can be a powerful lever to increase AOV. While offering free shipping across the board might not be feasible, setting a minimum order value to qualify for free shipping can drive customers to add that extra item to their cart. For instance, if free shipping kicks in at $50, a customer with $40 worth of goods in their cart might be tempted to add another $10 item instead of paying the shipping fee.

Educational marketing can also play a role in this. Providing detailed product guides, comparisons, and case studies can help customers understand the value of higher-priced or additional products. When you educate your customers, you empower them to make well-informed decisions, leading to higher satisfaction and increased spending.

Subscription models and auto-renewal options can guarantee a steady stream of revenue while also increasing the AOV over time. By offering products on a subscription basis, customers are likely to spend more on a recurring basis compared to one-time purchases. For instance, a monthly box of curated skincare products ensures that customers not only keep buying but also get to discover new items regularly, increasing their overall spend.

It's also worth exploring your checkout process. Simplifying and streamlining the checkout experience can prevent cart abandonment and encourage higher spends. Adding suggestions for last-minute purchases or bundling options at the checkout can lead to an easy and effective increase in the AOV.

Training your sales team effectively can't be overlooked either. In a physical retail setting, having knowledgeable and engaging staff who can suggest add-ons or upsells can significantly enhance the shopping experience and encourage higher spending. For instance, if a salesperson knows the inventory well, they can easily point out accessories or services that complement the customer's original purchase.

In this age of e-commerce and digital marketing, leveraging data analytics can give you insights into your customer's shopping habits and preferences, allowing you to tailor your strategies accordingly. Tracking metrics such as the average time between purchases, favorite product categories, and seasonal spending patterns can help you craft more targeted campaigns to boost AOV.

To sum it up, increasing your average order value doesn't just hinge on a single tactic but rather a blend of well-coordinated strategies. Each small increment in AOV can add up significantly over time, creating a compounding effect on your overall revenue. By focusing on delivering value to your customers, ensuring a great shopping experience, and strategically encouraging higher spends, you pave the way for optimizing your profit

CHAPTER 18: OPTIMIZING PROFIT MARGINS

margins effectively.

Chapter 19: Continuous Improvement

Continuous improvement isn't just a strategy; it's a mindset. Whether you're an entrepreneur hustling to hit your first million or a student figuring out your next steps, the key to growth is relentless refinement. It's about creating a culture where feedback is gold, learning from mistakes is celebrated, and iterative testing becomes second nature. Don't get comfortable; chase excellence by continually tweaking, testing, and improving every aspect of your business. Embrace change and be agile. This chapter is your guide to making incremental progress that leads to monumental success. So, keep pushing the envelope—because standing still is just not an option in a world that moves at breakneck speed.

Implementing Feedback

Implementing feedback effectively is crucial to achieving continuous improvement and ensuring your business's long-term success. It's more than just listening to opinions or ticking off boxes; it's about creating a culture where feedback is valued, analyzed, and acted upon in meaningful ways. In this section, we'll dive into why feedback is essential, how to solicit it, and most importantly, how to utilize it to propel your business forward.

First, let's understand the value of feedback. Think of feedback as a mirror that reflects both your strengths and weaknesses. It offers insights that you might not see otherwise. Whether it's a suggestion from a customer, advice from a mentor, or an observation from an employee, feedback is an invaluable asset. It can highlight blind spots and reveal opportunities for growth that you might miss if you're only relying on your own perspective. The end goal is simple: use feedback as a tool to make informed, data-driven decisions that will enhance your business.

So, how do you go about gathering this vital feedback? Start by creating multiple channels where feedback can pour in seamlessly. This can include surveys, social media polls, customer reviews, and direct conversations. Don't limit yourself to just one method; a diversified approach will give you a broader spectrum of insights. When asking for feedback, make it easy and convenient for people to share their thoughts. Simple, open-ended questions often yield the most valuable information. Instead of asking, "Did you like our product?" try, "What could we do to improve your experience?" This encourages more detailed responses that can provide actionable insights.

Once you've collected the feedback, the next step is analysis. Not all feedback is created equal; some comments will be more actionable than others. Look for patterns in the feedback you receive. Are multiple people mentioning the same issue or suggestion? These patterns can help you identify areas that need immediate attention. It's also crucial to prioritize the feedback based on its potential impact on your business. Some improvements might be quick wins, while others could require more significant resources and planning.

After analyzing the feedback, it's time to develop an action plan. This step might seem daunting, but it's where the magic happens. Start by categorizing feedback into different buckets, such as product improvements, customer service enhancements, and operational tweaks. Assign specific team members to tackle each category and set clear deadlines for implementation. It's also helpful to break down larger tasks into smaller, more manageable actions to ensure steady progress.

Transparency is key when it comes to implementing feedback. Keep your team and stakeholders informed about the changes you're making and the reasons behind them. This not only builds trust but also demonstrates that you value and act on the insights you receive. You might even consider sharing a "You Spoke, We Listened" update with your customers to show them that their input leads to real changes. This kind of transparency can significantly boost customer loyalty and engagement.

One of the most challenging aspects of implementing feedback is dealing with criticism. It's never easy to hear that something isn't working or that customers are unhappy. However, constructive criticism is one of the most powerful drivers of improvement. Approach negative feedback with an open mind and a commitment to finding solutions. Instead of taking criticism personally, view it as an opportunity to better your business. Always thank the person providing the feedback, regardless of its nature, to show that you appreciate their input.

It's also crucial to establish a continuous feedback loop. Implementing feedback shouldn't be a one-time effort but an ongoing process. Regularly solicit feedback, implement changes, and then seek feedback on those changes. This iterative cycle helps you stay agile and continuously improve your product or service. Regular feedback loops ensure that improvements are not just made but sustained over time. It also helps in keeping pace with changing customer expectations and market trends.

While customer feedback is invaluable, don't overlook internal feedback. Your employees are on the front lines and often have insights that can lead to significant improvements. Create a culture where team members feel comfortable voicing their opinions and suggestions. Regular team meetings, anonymous suggestion boxes, and one-on-one check-ins can all serve as excellent platforms for gathering internal feedback.

Integrating technology into your feedback implementation process can also be a game-changer. Customer Relationship Management (CRM) systems, feedback management tools, and analytics software can help you track, analyze, and act on feedback more efficiently. These tools can provide you with real-time insights and help you measure the impact of the changes you make. The more seamlessly integrated your feedback systems are, the more effective your continuous improvement efforts will be.

Let's not forget the importance of training and development in implementing feedback. Ensure your team is equipped with the skills and knowledge they need to act on feedback effectively. This might involve training sessions, workshops, or even bringing in external experts. The more empowered your team feels, the more proactive they will be in seeking and implementing feedback. Remember, continuous improvement is a collective effort that requires input and action from every member of your organization.

Lastly, celebrate your successes. When you implement feedback and see positive results, make sure to acknowledge and celebrate those achievements. It doesn't have to be a grand event; even small recognitions can go a long way in maintaining motivation and morale. Celebrating success not only encourages a positive feedback culture but also reinforces the value of continuous improvement within your organization.

In conclusion, implementing feedback is a powerful strategy for continuous improvement. It requires a systematic approach, from collecting and analyzing feedback to developing action plans and creating feedback loops. By valuing and acting on feedback, you're not only improving your product or service but also building a stronger, more resilient business. Always remember that feedback is a gift, and using it effectively is one of the most impactful ways to drive your business toward its first $1 million and beyond.

Iterative Testing

Iterative testing is all about experimentation and refinement. It's the pulse check on your business model that ensures everything is fine-tuned and fully optimized. You know that voice in your head that says, "Is this really the best way to do it?" Iterative testing answers with a resounding "Let's find out!" Think of it as your business's built-in scientist, constantly testing hypotheses and seeking evidence-based improvements.

Starting with a clear hypothesis is key. This isn't about random tweaks; it's a structured approach. Let's say you want to find out if changing the color of the 'Buy Now' button increases conversions. You hypothesize that a red button might perform better than a blue one due to its psychological impact. You then implement an A/B test, where both versions are shown to different segments of your audience simultaneously, and you observe which one performs better. It's meticulous, controlled, and heavily relies on data to make informed decisions.

And remember, it's not always going to yield the expected results. Sometimes, those wild guesses that seem like a shot in the dark turn out to be game-changers. Other times, the 'sure things' fall flat on their faces. That's the beauty of iterative testing—it's humbling but incredibly insightful. The goal is to constantly evolve, not to triumph every single time. Each test propels your understanding forward.

Now, you'll need the right tools to effectively carry out iterative testing. Platforms like Google Optimize, VWO, or even simpler tools like Google Analytics allow you to track metrics and compare results efficiently. But tools are only as good as the strategies behind them. This means focusing on what matters. Each iteration should have a specific metric, like click-through rate (CTR) or conversion rate, that directly impacts your bottom line. You're not just changing things for the sake of it; every alteration should have a clear objective behind it.

It's not just digital aspects of your business that benefit from this, either. Physical products go through rigorous iterative testing too. Ever heard of a minimum viable product (MVP)? It's the very first iteration of your product that's just good enough to be released to your early adopters. These users are gold mines of feedback. They tell you what works, what doesn't, and what could use a little tweaking. Their input becomes the cornerstone of your product's evolution. Never underestimate the power of listening to your customers—they're essentially doing the testing for you.

Feedback loops are another crucial aspect of iterative testing. Just as in scientific experiments, where you observe, hypothesize, experiment, analyze, and then repeat—your business should do the same. The cycle starts with collecting data from your current setup, whether it's website analytics, customer feedback, or sales figures. Next, you hypothesize what change could improve performance. This leads to experimentation, where you roll out the new variable in a controlled manner, followed by analyzing the results. This feedback then informs the next round of iteration.

It's also important to maintain agility during this process. Avoid getting too attached to a specific idea or method. It's crucial to remain open-minded and receptive to the data you're collecting. Sometimes, the iterative process reveals uncomfortable truths about your business or product that you'd

CHAPTER 19: CONTINUOUS IMPROVEMENT

rather not face, but addressing these head-on is what will ultimately lead to improvement and growth.

Let's talk about a real-world example. Take Dropbox, for instance. They started with a very basic MVP: a simple video that explained what they were building. This wasn't even a product yet, just an explanation of a concept. The feedback from that video helped them understand user pain points, which they used to refine their offering. They didn't just create a product and sit back. No, they constantly iterated—adding features, tweaking the user interface, and optimizing user experience based on continual testing and user feedback. This relentless pursuit of excellence through iterative testing led to massive growth and adoption.

For businesses at any stage, testing doesn't stop. Even when you think you have found the "perfect" solution, the market is continuously evolving. New competitors emerge, consumer preferences change, and technology advances. If you're not continually testing and iterating, you risk becoming obsolete. It's like being a shark—you have to keep moving to stay alive. The same principle applies to your business. You must keep testing, learning, and adapting.

Iterative testing is not limited to just your product or website; it can be applied to virtually every aspect of your business. Your marketing campaigns, for instance, can benefit immensely from this. Launching different versions of ad copy, experimenting with various headlines, or adjusting imagery based on audience segments—all these are forms of iterative testing. It allows you to see what resonates most with your audience and adjust accordingly.

It's also beneficial for team processes. Agile methodologies in project management are rooted in the same principles as iterative testing. They encourage small, incremental changes rather than massive, disruptive overhauls. By implementing these changes and gathering feedback swiftly, you can ensure that your team is always functioning at peak performance.

A practical tip: keep a detailed log of your iterations. Document what you changed, why you changed it, and what the results were. This record becomes incredibly valuable over time as it allows you to see patterns and avoid repeating mistakes. It's your business's diary of improvement, a tangible representation of your journey towards that first $1 million.

Iterative testing cultivates a culture of constant learning and improvement within your organization. Encourage your team to embrace this mindset. Make it clear that failures are simply data points on the path to success. Celebrate the wins but study the losses meticulously. Each iteration brings you one step closer to your goal.

To wrap up, iterative testing isn't a nice-to-have; it's a critical component of your business strategy. It's the backbone of continuous improvement, an ongoing process that ensures you're not just staying afloat but confidently steering towards success. Don't let fear of change or the unknown hold you back. Embrace the process, learn from each iteration, and you'll find yourself not just hitting milestones but consistently surpassing them.

Chapter 20: Crisis Management

Every business faces its share of crises, but it's how you handle them that sets you apart. Whether you're navigating an economic downturn or addressing negative feedback, staying calm and composed is your first step. A solid crisis management plan is imperative. You must be quick to identify the issue, communicate transparently with your team and customers, and implement solutions efficiently. Adaptability and resilience are key; this is your chance to recalibrate and emerge even stronger. Remember, a crisis often brings hidden opportunities. So, keep a cool head, stay focused on your goals, and use these moments to reinforce your strategies and refine your operations. Your ability to manage crises effectively can turn potential losses into remarkable gains.

Navigating Economic Downturns

An economic downturn can hit like an unexpected storm, but how you steer your ship through it can make all the difference. It's not just about survival; it's about positioning yourself to come out stronger. When the economy takes a nosedive, many businesses panic, and often, this panic leads to poor decisions. But you? You're going to be prepared.

One of the first steps in navigating an economic downturn is understanding that this isn't the end of the world, but a period of adjustment. Think of it as a wave you need to ride, rather than a wall you're going to crash into. Assess your financial health by meticulously examining your cash flow. Cash is king in times like these, and liquid assets are your best friend. Look for any liabilities that can be trimmed down. It's about being lean and mean, but without compromising the essence of your business.

During these times, maintaining strong liquidity is essential. It's easy to get overzealous when business is booming, but having an emergency fund isn't just for personal finances—it's crucial for your company too. Break down your budget and see where you can cut unnecessary expenses. Negotiate better terms with your suppliers or see if you can defer certain payments. Always communicate openly with your creditors; you'd be surprised at the leniency you can achieve just by asking.

Customer communication is critical, as the people who buy from you need reassurance that your business is stable. Reaching out through personalized messages can foster loyalty and ease any concerns they might have. Just because times are tough doesn't mean your customers will disappear. Adapt your messaging to the times. Acknowledge the situation and show empathy. Your customers will remember how you treated them during tough times.

Flexibility in your business model may be the ace up your sleeve. Can you offer payment plans, bundle deals, or additional services that play into the current economic sentiment? Look at market needs—what's suddenly in demand or what's declining? This adaptive approach can open new revenue streams you hadn't considered before. Flexibility can also mean tweaking your products to be more cost-effective both for you and your customers.

This is also the time to leverage technology to your utmost advantage. Cutting-edge tools can streamline operations, making your business more efficient. Automating routine tasks can reduce manpower requirements, freeing up your team to focus on more critical areas. But remember, technology is a tool. It's still your strategies and decisions steering the ship. So don't skimp on training your team to make the most out of these tools.

Your marketing budget shouldn't be the first on the chopping block. However, how you allocate that budget may need to change. Focus on cost-effective methods like social media marketing and content marketing. These platforms aren't just affordable; they're effective means of staying connected with your audience. The goal is to keep your brand visible without bleeding money.

CHAPTER 20: CRISIS MANAGEMENT

Innovation during an economic downturn might seem counterintuitive, but often it's a necessity. When the usual avenues of revenue start drying up, new ideas are needed to keep things flowing. Encourage your team to think outside the box, and don't be afraid to pivot if a promising new idea comes along. History has shown that necessitated innovation during tough times can lead to breakthroughs.

Let's not forget the human element—your team. The morale of your employees is your hidden asset. Open communication is more vital than ever. Transparency about the company's situation can build trust and motivate your team to rally. This is not just about leading but inspiring. Offer flexibility where possible, such as remote work options or mental health days. Your team's productivity is tied to their well-being.

Lastly, invest in yourself during this time. Economic downturns are not just about your business; they're about personal growth too. Use this period to broaden your skill set or deepen your knowledge in an area relevant to your business. Whether it's online courses, certifications, or even reading books and keeping up with industry news, be proactive about your personal development. As you grow, you equip yourself with new perspectives and solutions that could be the game-changer for your business.

In conclusion, navigating an economic downturn is about balance—maintaining liquidity while keeping your team motivated and your customers engaged. It's about being flexible but clear-eyed. Cash flow, customer communication, efficient technology use, and innovating can help you not only survive an economic downturn but thrive in it. The principles you establish now will build resilience and prepare you for any future challenges that come your way.

Handling Negative Feedback

When you're on the road to hitting your first $1 million, you'll inevitably encounter negative feedback. It can sting, but it's a critical part of growing and refining your business. Negative feedback is essentially a goldmine of information, once you learn how to mine it effectively. Think of it as constructive criticism that can lead to constructive action. It's not always easy, but handling it well can turn a potentially damaging situation into a valuable learning opportunity.

First off, don't take it personally. Negative feedback about your business is not an indictment of you as a person. Separate your identity from your business. This separation allows you to handle critical feedback more rationally and less emotionally. Easier said than done, right? It takes practice, but the more you can cultivate this mindset, the better.

Listen actively. When negative feedback rolls in, your first instinct might be to defend yourself or your business. Resist the urge. Listen to what is being said. Sometimes, customers just want to know they're being heard. Acknowledging their concerns can go a long way in mending relationships and showing that you value their input. This approach doesn't mean you have to agree with everything they say, but it does set the stage for constructive dialogue.

After listening, take a step back and analyze the feedback objectively. Gather all the negative feedback you receive, and look for common themes. Is there a consistent issue that multiple customers are pointing out? This could be an indication of a systemic problem that needs addressing. Fixing these underlying issues can save you headaches and money in the long run.

Now, let's be clear: not all feedback is created equal. Some feedback might be utterly unreasonable and driven by factors beyond your control. It's up to you to discern which critiques are actionable and which are outliers. Engage in a triage process: categorize feedback into what's actionable, what's relevant but not urgent, and what's not worth your time. This helps you prioritize and manage your responses efficiently.

Once you've decided on actionable feedback, communicate your plans to address it. Notify the customer, either individually or through a public platform, about the steps you're taking to remedy the issue. Transparency is key here. It builds trust and shows that you're committed to improving. Remember, your customers are your stakeholders in a sense, and keeping them informed can bolster their confidence in your business.

Swift action is paramount. The quicker you can turn feedback into action, the better. For instance, if multiple customers critique the functionality of your website, don't sit on this feedback. Get your tech team on it immediately. A prompt response not only mends customer relationships but also shows your broader audience that you are a responsive and responsible business owner.

It can also be valuable to create a feedback loop within your company. Encourage your team to share the negative feedback they encounter and brainstorm collective solutions. This approach fosters a culture of continuous improvement and helps identify potential issues before they escalate. It's not just about dealing with the feedback at hand but preventing similar feedback in the future.

Use the feedback as a learning tool to train your team. Real-world examples of what went wrong and how it was fixed can serve as case studies for employee training. This way, your entire team becomes more adept at handling and preventing negative feedback, amplifying your ability to provide stellar customer service.

Engage directly with customers who provided the feedback. Personal interaction can turn a negative experience into a positive one. A quick phone call, personalized email, or even a face-to-face meeting can work wonders. This is your chance to turn a critic into a loyal customer, and maybe even an advocate for your brand. People appreciate authenticity and effort, and a personal touch can make all the difference.

Use social media wisely. Bad reviews and negative comments can spread like wildfire on social platforms, but they also offer an opportunity to showcase your customer service skills publicly. Respond promptly and professionally to negative comments on social media. Address the issues and outline the steps you're taking to resolve them. This not only helps the individual customer but also shows potential customers your commitment to quality and care.

However, be wary of online trolls. Some individuals thrive on creating chaos online. It's essential to recognize when engagement is futile. In cases involving trolls, it might be best to simply document the feedback and consult with your PR team on the appropriate steps forward, possibly involving the platform's moderation tools.

Document your responses for future reference. Keeping a log of feedback and the actions taken to resolve issues can be an invaluable resource. It helps you track patterns over time and measure the effectiveness of your responses. This documentation can also serve as a training tool for onboarding new team members or refining your feedback management processes.

Incorporate this documented feedback into your strategic planning. Use it as a guide to steer product development, customer service protocols, and marketing strategies. The goal is not just to fix what went wrong but to proactively improve your business to prevent future negative feedback.

Celebrate the wins. When you turn negative feedback into a success story, don't forget to celebrate it with your team. Recognize the efforts of those who contributed to turning the situation around. This not only boosts morale but also reinforces the importance of handling negative feedback constructively.

Every piece of negative feedback can be a stepping stone to improvement. The key is to handle it with grace, act swiftly, and learn from the experience. Remember, your journey to $1 million will have its ups and downs, and how you handle the rough patches can make all the difference.

Chapter 21: Long-term Sustainability

Creating a long-term sustainable business goes beyond just hitting sales targets and quarterly goals. It's about building a community that believes in your vision and embraces your brand. Think about the future and plan accordingly – what does your business look like five, ten, or twenty years from now? Diversify your revenue streams and invest in research and development to stay ahead of the curve. Engage with your customers regularly, adapting to their evolving needs while staying true to your core values. Remember, sustainability isn't just environmental; it's financial and operational resilience that ensures you can weather any storm and keep thriving. Strategically reinvesting profits and fostering a culture that values innovation and adaptability can go a long way in making sure your venture stands the test of time.

Building a Community

Building a community isn't just a nice-to-have; it's essential for the long-term sustainability of your business. Think about it: would you be more loyal to a brand where you feel at home, or one where you're just another customer? Exactly. Creating a community around your brand is an art that pays off in dividends, often in ways you can't initially quantify. It's about forming connections, offering value, and creating a sense of belonging. When people feel like part of something bigger, they stick around.

The first step in building a community is to identify the common values and needs that bind your audience together. This could be a shared passion, a common goal, or even similar struggles. You want to tap into those elements to create a space where people can connect over their mutual interests. Think of it like hosting a party but every guest has a reason to be there and something to contribute. Your role is the host, making sure everyone feels welcomed and valued.

Start by leveraging your existing customer base. These are people who already believe in your product or service, so they are natural allies in your community-building efforts. Send out surveys, host focus groups, or even casual meet-ups to learn more about what makes them tick. By understanding their needs and desires, you can tailor your community initiatives to meet them where they are. Plus, involving them in the process makes them feel valued and heard.

Once you've gathered these insights, you can begin the task of creating a platform for your community. This could be a Facebook group, a forum on your website, or even a series of local events. The key here is accessibility and consistency. People should be able to easily engage with one another and with your brand. Regular updates, engaging content, and prompt responses to queries will keep the community vibrant and active.

Now, you might be thinking, "This sounds like a lot of work!" And you're right. Building a community requires effort and dedication. However, the returns are well worth it. A strong community reduces customer churn, enhances brand loyalty, and even turns members into brand advocates. These advocates can help spread the word about your brand, bringing in new customers at little to no cost to you.

Another powerful tool in building a community is user-generated content. Encourage members to share their experiences, reviews, photos, or even creative works related to your brand. This not only provides fresh content but also gives the community a sense of ownership. When people see their contributions recognized, they feel a deeper connection to the brand and are more likely to engage actively.

Speaking of engagement, don't shy away from interactions. Host live Q&A sessions, webinars, or panels featuring experts in your industry. These events can provide immense value, educate your audience, and position your brand

CHAPTER 21: LONG-TERM SUSTAINABILITY

as a thought leader. Plus, they're a fantastic way to get real-time feedback and insights.

Your community should also have a clear set of guidelines and values. This helps maintain a positive and respectful environment where everyone feels safe to share and participate. These guidelines should be enforced consistently to avoid any form of toxicity, which can quickly erode the sense of belonging you've worked so hard to build.

Nurture your community by recognizing and rewarding active members. Shoutouts, exclusive offers, and even small tokens of appreciation can go a long way in making members feel special. People love to be acknowledged, and it can motivate them to contribute even more. You can also create special roles or titles within the community to add a sense of hierarchy and accomplishment.

Remember, a community is a two-way street. It's not just about what you can get from your members, but also what you can give them. Regularly ask for their input and take their feedback seriously. Implement changes based on their suggestions when feasible and let them know they had a hand in shaping the brand. This collaborative approach not only strengthens the community but also improves your business.

Building a community requires time and patience. It's not something that happens overnight. However, the benefits of having a loyal, engaged community are immense. They can help you weather tough times, provide invaluable insights, and act as the bedrock of your business's long-term sustainability. While the initial investment may seem daunting, the payoff both in terms of emotional and financial ROI is well worth it.

So, as you focus on the big picture and aim for that first $1 million, don't underestimate the power of a robust community. It's not just about individual transactions but cultivating relationships that will sustain and grow with your business over time. A thriving community is an asset that, once established, can become a self-sustaining ecosystem of support, loyalty, and advocacy. By building a community, you're not just creating customers; you're creating die-hard fans who will stand by you through thick and thin.

Planning for the Future

Looking past the immediate goals and envisioning your future is essential for long-term sustainability in business. It's easy to get caught up in the hustle and bustle of meeting quarterly targets or launching new products, but planning for what lies beyond is what sets thriving businesses apart from those that merely survive. Your journey to the first $1 million is a landmark moment, but it's just the foundation for what comes next.

You've got to ask yourself, "Where does this business need to go in five, ten, or even twenty years from now?" This question isn't just philosophical; it's practical. By forecasting, you create a roadmap that guides your decisions today. Think of future planning as setting up a chessboard. Each move should align with your long-term strategy. Building resilience into your business model now will prepare you for whatever comes next.

Baking flexibility into your plans allows you to adapt as the market changes. When you establish systems that can evolve, you ensure that your business won't be left behind as new technologies emerge or consumer behaviors shift. This kind of agility isn't an afterthought—it's integral to long-term success.

Invest in research and development to stay ahead of trends. This often means dedicating a portion of your budget to innovative projects and ensuring that your team is constantly learning and adapting. While it's tempting to put all resources toward immediate revenue-generating activities, innovation is the fuel that will drive your long-term sustainability engine.

Developing new revenue streams is another cornerstone of future planning. If your business relies on a single product or market, you're vulnerable to shifts that are outside of your control. Diversify your offerings and explore ways to expand your market base. This not only stabilizes your revenue, but opens up new avenues for growth.

But remember, future planning isn't just about broad strokes; it involves meticulous attention to detail. Scenario planning can prove invaluable. Imagine various scenarios—best case, worst case, and everything in between—and strategize your response to each. This exercise can reveal vulnerabilities in your current plan and prepare you for quick pivots when necessary.

CHAPTER 21: LONG-TERM SUSTAINABILITY

Building a resilient financial foundation is also critical. You need a clear financial strategy that forecasts cash flow needs and identifies potential investment opportunities. Ensure your financial planning is robust enough to withstand unexpected downturns or opportunities that require immediate capital outlay. This includes keeping an emergency fund and having access to lines of credit.

An often-overlooked aspect of planning for the future is team development. Your people are your greatest asset. Investing in their growth, offering continuous learning opportunities, and fostering a culture of innovation will pay long-term dividends. Encourage a forward-thinking mindset at every level of your organization.

While technology can be a game-changer, remember that it's just a tool. How you leverage technology will determine its impact on your business. Cloud computing, AI, machine learning, and blockchain are already shaping industries. Keep up with technological advancements and consider how they can be integrated into your business model for improved efficiency and scalability.

Part of future planning involves protecting your intellectual property. As your business grows and evolves, so does the potential for IP-related issues. Regularly review your patents, trademarks, and copyrights to ensure they're up-to-date and fully protect your innovations.

Another crucial component is building a robust network. Networking shouldn't be a transactional or short-term endeavor. Surround yourself with mentors, advisors, and peers who can offer long-term support and guidance. These relationships can provide insights that might not be readily apparent from within your organization.

Your brand will also need to evolve. Maintaining a consistent brand message while adapting to new market trends is a delicate balance. As you plan for the future, think about how your brand can maintain its core values while resonating with future consumer bases. It might be beneficial to periodically reassess your brand strategy to ensure it aligns with your long-term goals.

Planning for the future isn't all about tangible actions; it also involves a shift in mindset. Foster an environment that rewards forward-thinking and calculated risk-taking. Encourage your team to question the status quo and look for new opportunities. In doing so, you create a culture that's not only poised for growth but also resilient in the face of adversity.

Incorporate sustainability practices into your long-term plan. Consumers and stakeholders are increasingly valuing businesses that operate responsibly. Address environmental, social, and governance (ESG) factors in your planning. Whether it's reducing your carbon footprint or enhancing community engagement, sustainable practices can boost your brand value and customer loyalty.

Don't shy away from revisiting and revising your plans. Annual reviews are a must. These aren't just perfunctory exercises—they are critical checkpoints. Use these reviews to assess progress, make necessary adjustments, and ensure that your long-term vision remains relevant. Agile planning enables you to adapt strategies based on the latest market intelligence and performance data.

Finally, remember that you don't have to go it alone. Leverage your network, advisors, and other resources. Sometimes, seeking external expertise can provide insights and strategies that you might overlook. Whether it's through consultancies, mentorship, or peer groups, tapping into external knowledge can be a key differentiator.

Planning for the future demands a delicate balance of aspiration and pragmatism. It's an ongoing process that requires you to be both a visionary and a realist. By continuously refining your long-term strategies, investing in innovation, and fostering a resilient organizational culture, you set the stage for sustained success and exponential growth. The next million is just a milestone—let your vision for the future be the guiding light that ensures your business thrives for decades to come.

Chapter 22: Networking and Mentorship

As you navigate the challenging and rewarding journey toward your first $1 million, never underestimate the power of networking and mentorship. Building relationships with experienced mentors can offer invaluable insights, guiding you through obstacles and helping you capitalize on opportunities you might've otherwise missed. Seek out networking events, professional groups, and online communities where you can connect with like-minded individuals. Mentors can provide not only advice but also introductions to key industry players and potential clients. Remember, sometimes, it's not just what you know, but who you know, that makes the difference. Invest time in nurturing these relationships; it'll pay dividends in your business growth and personal development.

Finding Mentors

Finding mentors can be a game-changer for any entrepreneur. It's not just about having a sounding board; it's about accessing years of experience, sidestepping common pitfalls, and benefiting from a seasoned perspective. Imagine trotting along a road on your way to your first million and suddenly, you have someone who's been there, done that, guiding your every step. That's the power of mentorship.

Now, the first thing you need to understand is that mentors don't just fall from the sky. You have to be proactive. Think of it like dating—you've got to put yourself out there. Start by identifying what you need. Are you struggling with product development? Could your financial management skills use some brushing up? Make a list of the areas where you feel you need guidance. This will help you find mentors who align with your goals.

Once you've identified your needs, it's time to look for potential mentors. Start with your existing network—friends, family, colleagues. You'd be surprised how many connections you already have. Next, make use of online platforms like LinkedIn. It's not just for job hunting or posting work anniversaries. Use it to connect with industry leaders, join relevant groups, and participate in discussions. Be sure to personalize your connection requests; tell them why you want to connect and what you hope to learn from them.

Don't underestimate the power of local networking events and industry conferences either. Face-to-face interactions can create a strong bond. When you're at these events, don't just focus on collecting business cards. Engage in meaningful conversations. Ask questions, share your vision, and be genuine. People can smell desperation from a mile away, so make sure your interactions come off as authentic.

Alright, so let's say you've pinpointed a few potential mentors. How do you approach them? The key is to be respectful and to demonstrate that you're worth their time. Start with a brief, respectful email or message. Introduce yourself, explain why you admire their work, and specify what kind of help you're looking for. It's crucial to keep it concise. Nobody wants to read through a novel-length email.

For example, you could write something like: "Hi [Mentor's Name], My name is [Your Name], and I'm currently working on building [brief description of your venture]. I've been following your work on [specific project or general expertise], and I'm particularly inspired by [specific aspect]. I would be incredibly grateful for the opportunity to learn from you. Would you be open to a short chat over coffee or a call?"

Once you've secured a mentor, it's essential to make the most out of the relationship. Always come prepared for your meetings. Have specific questions or issues you want to discuss. Take notes, and more importantly, take their advice seriously. There's nothing more discouraging to a mentor than giving advice that goes unheeded. It's a mutual relationship; their

CHAPTER 22: NETWORKING AND MENTORSHIP

success is tied to your success, so respect their time and expertise.

As your business grows, your needs will evolve, and so might your mentors. It's perfectly okay to have multiple mentors for different facets of your business. Also, don't forget to give back. Offer to help your mentors with their projects or introduce them to valuable contacts. A mentor-mentee relationship is symbiotic; both parties should benefit.

Another source of mentorship can be through mentorship programs and incubators. Many organizations offer formal mentorship programs where you're paired with industry veterans. These programs often provide structured guidance and accountability. Look into startup incubators and accelerators as well. They usually come with a built-in mentorship component, and being part of one can also expand your network significantly.

Books, podcasts, and webinars can also be supplementary mentors. Sure, they can't offer personalized advice, but they are packed with wisdom. Find books written by successful entrepreneurs in your field. Listen to podcasts where industry experts dissect challenges similar to yours. Webinars often provide Q&A sessions where you can get some of your specific questions answered.

In the end, finding a mentor is less about a single grand gesture and more about sustained effort and being genuinely committed to learning and growing. The journey to your first million will have its fair share of ups and downs, but with a good mentor by your side, you will navigate it more gracefully and effectively.

Remember, it's not about finding a perfect mentor but finding someone who understands your challenges and can provide valuable insights to help you grow. Don't be afraid to reach out and ask for guidance. Successful people are often more willing to help than you think; they too were once where you are now. With the right mentors, the road to your first million becomes a collaborative, insightful, and highly rewarding path.

Building Your Network

If you've ever watched a pro sports team win a championship, you'll know it's not just about one star player. It takes a full roster, coaches, and often, some skilled and passionate fans cheering them on. The same holds true for your entrepreneurial journey. Building a network is about surrounding yourself with the right people who can amplify your efforts, advise you during tough times, and even share opportunities you wouldn't have seen on your own.

Your network isn't just about quantity; it's about quality. Sure, having a huge list of contacts may seem impressive, but if none of these people can add value or guide you in your journey, it's essentially just a vanity metric. Focus instead on developing relationships with people who align with your vision and whose skills and experiences complement yours.

So, where do you start? Begin with the low-hanging fruit: your current circle. These are your friends, family, colleagues, and acquaintances. They already know you, and most are likely willing to help you in some way. This doesn't mean you should go asking everyone for favors. Instead, engage them in meaningful conversations about your goals and challenges. You might be surprised at the kind of assistance you'll receive, from advice and introductions to actual resources you need.

Next, leverage social media to your advantage. Platforms like LinkedIn, Twitter, and even Instagram can be powerful tools for networking if used strategically. Start by optimizing your profiles to highlight your entrepreneurial journey and your vision. Post regularly about your progress, share valuable content, and engage with others in your industry. When approaching new contacts, be genuine. Personalized messages that show you've done your homework can set you apart from those who spam generic requests.

Attending events, both online and offline, is another crucial strategy. Industry conferences, workshops, and seminars offer the perfect setting to meet like-minded individuals and potential mentors. These venues are filled with people who are also looking to grow their networks. Don't just collect business cards—aim to build actual relationships. Follow up with the

CHAPTER 22: NETWORKING AND MENTORSHIP

people you meet, and find ways to add value to them. A useful introduction or a bit of advice can go a long way in cementing a new relationship.

Remember, networking isn't about making transactional connections; it's about building genuine relationships. The best networking relationships are those where both parties benefit mutually. Think about how you can help others in your network achieve their goals. Sometimes, paying it forward can lead to unexpected opportunities and alliances down the road.

An often-overlooked aspect of networking is the importance of mentors. While your network can provide a broad base of support, mentors offer focused, high-impact guidance tailored to your specific needs. Identifying potential mentors can make a huge difference in your career. Look for individuals who have achieved what you aim to accomplish and who are willing to share their insights with you. Approach them respectfully and show them why you value their time and expertise.

Engage in community service and join industry-specific groups and organizations. Volunteering for a cause you care about not only makes a positive impact on your community but also broadens your network in meaningful ways. You get to meet people outside your immediate industry, diversify your contacts, and often find inspiration from unexpected places.

Don't underestimate the power of your alma mater. Most universities have strong alumni networks that are eager to support fellow graduates. Reach out to your alumni association, attend reunions, and participate in alumni events. This can be an excellent way to connect with people who share a common background and are more likely to be willing to help.

Consistency is the backbone of effective networking. It's not enough to make contact once and then disappear. Follow-up and regular engagement are crucial. Schedule periodic check-ins with your contacts, send updates about your journey, and stay in touch. This helps keep your relationship warm and your network active.

Lastly, stay open to serendipity. Some of your most valuable connections will come from unexpected places, like a casual conversation at a coffee shop or a seatmate on a flight. Always be open to meeting new people and exploring new avenues. You never know where the next great opportunity will come from.

In conclusion, building your network is not a one-time task; it's an ongoing effort. It requires time, intentionality, and a lot of consistency. But the payoff is well worth the investment. The right network can provide support, open doors to opportunities, and accelerate your path to success. So roll up your sleeves, start making meaningful connections, and watch both your network and your success grow.

Chapter 23: Legal and Compliance

In the pursuit of your first million, it's critical not to overlook the legal and compliance aspects of your business. Being proactive in understanding regulations that pertain to your industry can save you from costly fines and legal issues down the road. This doesn't just mean reading up on laws; it involves actively protecting your intellectual property, whether it's trademarks, patents, or copyrights. Remember, a well-protected business is a sustainable one. Take the time to consult with legal professionals who can guide you through the complexities of compliance and help establish a solid legal foundation. By doing so, you're not just safeguarding your business but also building trust with your customers and stakeholders, which is invaluable as you scale.

Understanding Regulations

Let's dive straight into one of the critical, yet often overlooked, pillars of your entrepreneurial journey: understanding regulations. It might not be the most glamorous part of building a business, but trust me, it's essential. Navigating the maze of laws and regulations can be daunting, but it's a journey you don't have to undertake alone. Think of this section as your roadmap.

First and foremost, why are regulations so crucial? Well, they help ensure that your business operates fairly and legally, protecting you, your customers, and your stakeholders. From registering your business to adhering to industry-specific guidelines, compliance is non-negotiable. Ignoring this can lead to fines, lawsuits, or even the shutting down of your business. It's like playing a game; you need to know the rules to win.

It's tempting to skip over the fine print when you're excited about launching your product or service. However, legal and regulatory issues touch almost every aspect of your business. From employment laws that affect your hiring practices to tax regulations that impact your bottom line, legal compliance is an integral part of maintaining a healthy business. Take it seriously, and you'll sidestep a lot of headaches down the road.

One of the primary steps in understanding regulations is knowing what type of business structure you're going for. Will you be a sole proprietor, a partnership, an LLC, or a corporation? Each structure comes with its own set of legal requirements and implications. For instance, an LLC offers more protection against personal liability compared to a sole proprietorship. Choosing the right structure is crucial for both your legal safety and financial strategies.

Once you've decided on your business structure, the next step is registering your business. This usually involves filling out forms and paying a fee, but it also includes selecting a unique name for your business that complies with state or local guidelines. Make sure to research the naming regulations in your jurisdiction; the last thing you want is to find out your dream business name is already taken or restricted.

Permits and licenses are another vital aspect of business regulations. Depending on your industry and location, you may need various permits to operate legally. These can include health permits, zoning permits, and even special licenses for certain professions. It's essential to check with local, state, and federal agencies to ensure you're not missing any crucial permits. Ignorance won't get you off the hook if you're found operating without the necessary approvals.

Regulations are not just about keeping you in line; they also offer protections. For instance, the Fair Labor Standards Act (FLSA) ensures that you pay your employees fairly, which can protect you from wage disputes. The Equal Employment Opportunity (EEO) laws provide guidelines for non-discriminatory hiring practices, helping you foster a more inclusive workplace. Following these regulations can actually be a competitive advantage, making

CHAPTER 23: LEGAL AND COMPLIANCE

your business more attractive to top talent.

Intellectual property (IP) protection is another crucial area of regulatory compliance. This covers things like trademarks, copyrights, and patents. Ensuring your creative ideas, innovations, and brand identifiers are legally protected provides you a competitive edge. It prevents competitors from stealing your hard work and safeguards your business's unique aspects.

Data protection and privacy regulations are becoming increasingly vital as businesses move online. Laws such as the General Data Protection Regulation (GDPR) in Europe have severe penalties for non-compliance. Even if you're based in the U.S., if you have European customers, you need to comply. Understanding regulations around data protection can save you from hefty fines and help build customer trust.

Tax compliance is another critical area where many entrepreneurs falter. From sales tax to income tax, understanding your tax obligations is essential for financial stability. Hire a good accountant or financial advisor who can guide you through the complexities of tax laws. Don't procrastinate on tax obligations; they can accumulate and lead to severe financial strain.

With e-commerce on the rise, there are additional regulations specific to online businesses. These can range from regulations on advertising and marketing to rules around digital transactions. Make sure you are compliant with the Federal Trade Commission (FTC) guidelines on online advertising. Transparency with your customers not only adheres to the law but can also build brand loyalty.

If you are planning to export or import goods, there are international trade regulations to consider. These laws can be incredibly complex, covering everything from tariffs to product labeling requirements. Make sure you're well-versed in the regulations governing the countries you're doing business with. Export assistance centers and international trade consultants can be invaluable resources.

Another layer of complexity comes with environmental regulations. If your business impacts the environment, you'll need to comply with laws designed to protect air quality, water resources, and more. These laws vary widely depending on your industry and location, so it's wise to consult an environmental law expert.

Lastly, let's talk about ongoing compliance. Laws and regulations are not static; they evolve over time. Keeping up-to-date with changes in relevant laws is a continuous process. It's a good idea to set up regular check-ins with your legal advisor to make sure you're always on the right side of the law.

Understanding regulations may seem overwhelming, but breaking it down into manageable pieces helps. You're not expected to know everything, but you should know where to look and when to seek expert advice. In the end, being proactive about legal and regulatory requirements can save you from a lot of potential pitfalls, helping you focus more on growing your business.

Intellectual Property Protection

Intellectual property (IP) protection is often one of those overlooked areas that can mean the difference between thriving and surviving in today's competitive landscape. As you journey towards your first $1 million, it's essential to not only recognize the value of your ideas but also to protect them. Think of IP protection as an insurance policy on your creativity and hard work. You wouldn't leave your front door unlocked, right? The same logic should apply to your business assets.

First things first, let's break down what we mean by intellectual property. IP is a broad term that covers the creations of your mind. This can include inventions, designs, original works of authorship, and even symbols or names used in commerce. Your product idea, the brand name you've brainstormed, the unique logo, and even your website content—all these are forms of intellectual property. Protecting these assets can provide you with a competitive edge and financial benefits, especially when it's time to scale or sell your business.

Now, what are the different types of IP protection you should be aware of? Let's go over the big four: patents, trademarks, copyrights, and trade secrets. Understanding these will help you decide which form of protection is appropriate for your business.

Patents are all about protecting inventions. If you've come up with a unique product or a novel way of doing something, a patent can keep competitors at bay for up to 20 years. To get a patent, you'll need to disclose how your invention works, which can be a double-edged sword. Yes, you get protection, but you're also revealing your secret sauce. Nevertheless, in many industries, patents are vital. Major tech companies and pharmaceutical firms rely heavily on them.

Trademarks, on the other hand, protect brand elements like names, slogans, and logos. They ensure that your customers can distinguish your products from those of your competitors. Imagine, after building a successful brand, discovering a slew of cheap knock-offs using a similar name. A federally registered trademark could prevent this scenario and also elevate your brand's perceived legitimacy and value.

Then we have copyrights, which safeguard original works of authorship. This type of protection is essential if your business deals with content creation. From blog posts and marketing materials to software code and instructional videos, copyrights help protect against unauthorized copying and distribution of your work. Copyrights are automatically in force the moment your original work is created and fixed in a tangible medium, but registering them provides additional benefits in enforcement.

Trade secrets are a little different. Instead of registering your secret recipe or proprietary method, you keep it under wraps with strong confidentiality agreements. Think of the Coca-Cola formula or Google's search algorithm. These trade secrets can offer protection indefinitely, as long as the secret is maintained. Unlike patents, trade secrets don't require public disclosure, letting you keep your competitive edge hidden from prying eyes.

Alright, so how do you actually go about securing this protection? Well, it's a bit of a journey. Start with proper documentation. For patents, you'll need detailed descriptions and diagrams of your invention. For trademarks, collect samples of your brand elements and document their usage. Copyright registration can be done through the U.S. Copyright Office with ease. And for trade secrets, make sure you have rock-solid non-disclosure agreements (NDAs) and confidentiality policies in place.

It's advisable to consult with an IP attorney to navigate the nuances of intellectual property law. Yes, this will cost you some money upfront, but it's an investment in your business's future. A good attorney can help you assess which forms of protection suit your needs and guide you through the registration process. They can also perform a clearance search to ensure your proposed trademark or patent doesn't infringe on an existing one, saving you from potential legal headaches down the line.

But what happens if someone infringes on your IP? That's where enforcement comes in. You'll need to be proactive about monitoring the marketplace for potential violations. Tools like Google Alerts can help you keep tabs on any unauthorized use of your brand names or content. If you do discover an infringement, your legal team can send a cease-and-desist letter as a first step. Most of the time, this is enough to resolve the issue. If it's not, you may need to escalate to litigation, which can be complex and costly, but necessary to protect your interests.

As you move forward, remember that IP protection isn't a one-time task but an ongoing commitment. Regularly review and update your IP portfolio. As your business evolves, new products and ideas will emerge, and they'll need their own protection strategies. Additionally, keep an eye on the expiration dates of your patents and trademarks, and be prepared to renew them if they continue to hold value for your business.

One last thing to note is the importance of international IP protection if you plan on scaling globally. Different countries have different IP laws, and protections in the U.S. won't necessarily cover you overseas. Consider using services like the Madrid Protocol for trademarks or the Patent Cooperation Treaty (PCT) for patents to simplify international filing processes.

In conclusion, protecting your intellectual property is vital for maintaining your competitive advantage and ensuring the longevity of your business. It's like securing the foundation upon which your business is built. With proper IP protection, you can confidently grow, innovate, and thrive, knowing that your hard work and creativity are legally safeguarded. So take that step, seek the necessary legal assistance, and give your business the best possible chance for success.

Chapter 24: Innovation and Evolution

As you approach the critical juncture between steady growth and explosive potential, innovation and evolution become your lifeline. Picture your business as a dynamic entity—always needing to stay ahead of trends and adapt to market changes. It's not just about having the next big idea, but also about fostering a culture that's always ready to pivot, experiment, and learn. Whether you're integrating cutting-edge technology, tweaking your product lines, or responding to shifting customer needs, the ability to innovate isn't optional; it's essential. Embrace change, encourage creativity within your team, and never let your business rest on its laurels. This continuous cycle of evolution keeps you not only relevant but also ahead of the competition, setting the stage for sustained success and long-term growth.

Staying Ahead of Trends

In the fast-paced world of business, "staying ahead of trends" isn't just a buzzphrase—it's a lifeline. In the context of innovation and evolution, being ahead of the curve is like having a compass in the wilderness. It gives you direction and prepares you for what lies beyond the horizon. Every successful entrepreneur and business owner will tell you that one key to sustaining growth is anticipating market shifts before they hit the mainstream.

So, how do you keep your finger on the pulse? First, immerse yourself in the ecosystem of your industry. Follow thought leaders and subscribe to relevant publications and podcasts. But don't just stop there. Engage in discussions on platforms like LinkedIn and Twitter. These activities are like tuning into a live broadcast of your industry's heartbeat.

But awareness can only get you so far. Being proactive is equally crucial. Simply knowing about a trend isn't enough; you need to act on it. Let's say you notice that customers are increasingly interested in environmentally-friendly products. Don't just take note—consider how you can incorporate sustainable practices into your operation. Can you source eco-friendly materials or adopt greener methods for shipping? Taking these steps can put you ahead of competitors who are slow to adapt.

Identifying the "next big thing" often means listening to your customers. Collect feedback religiously and analyze it. What are their pain points? What solutions are they desperately seeking that the market hasn't yet fulfilled? Imagine if you were the first to offer what everyone didn't realize they wanted yet. Customer insights can be a goldmine for staying ahead of trends.

Here's where it also pays to be a bit of a futurist. Technologies like artificial intelligence, blockchain, and virtual reality may seem cutting-edge now, but they're already influencing many industries. Look for ways to integrate these technologies into your business. Imagine the possibilities of using AI to personalize customer experiences or blockchain for secure transaction verifications. The sky's the limit when you're willing to experiment with emerging tech.

Travel can also broaden your perspective. Visiting different parts of the world exposes you to new practices, products, and consumer behaviors. What's hot in Tokyo might not yet be on anyone's radar in New York. Global trends often filter down to local markets, so why not be the one to introduce them? Attending international conferences and trade shows can give you unique insights and open up opportunities that local competitors might miss.

And speaking of competition, always keep an eye on them. But don't just imitate—innovate. Reverse engineering—analyzing the steps competitors took to be successful—can be educational. Yet, it's the unique spin or additional value you offer that will truly set you apart. Think about what you can do differently or better.

Every now and then, revisit your business model. Is it still the best it can

CHAPTER 24: INNOVATION AND EVOLUTION

be? Are there pivot options that you haven't considered? Kodak is a prime example of a company that rested on its laurels while digital photography revolutionized the industry. Don't be a Kodak. Be willing to pivot if it means staying relevant.

Also, consider leveraging data analytics. In today's digital age, data isn't just numbers; it's a narrative. Employ tools and software that can help you analyze consumer behavior, sales patterns, and market dynamics. Effective use of data can reveal trends even before they become apparent to the naked eye.

Flexibility is another critical factor. The ability to adapt is woven into the fabric of staying ahead. Market landscapes can change in an instant. Stay agile enough to shift your strategies and operations as needed. Being rigid in your approach can lead you down a path to obsolescence.

Cultivating a culture of innovation within your organization can't be overstated. Empower your team to brainstorm and encourage out-of-the-box thinking. Sometimes the most groundbreaking ideas come from unexpected places. Fostering an environment where innovation thrives can give your business a continuous edge.

Networking is another pillar. Connect with other forward-thinkers across different industries. Cross-industry insights can be incredibly valuable. Sometimes ideas from completely unrelated fields can spark the next big thing in your own industry. Join mastermind groups, attend seminars, and never miss an opportunity to learn from others.

Lastly, never underestimate the power of education. Encourage lifelong learning within your team as well as for yourself. Whether it's through online courses, workshops, or formal education, keeping those mental gears turning will help you stay adaptable and ahead of trends.

Ultimately, staying ahead of trends isn't a one-time effort but an ongoing commitment. It's about cultivating a mindset that thrives on curiosity, innovation, and a willingness to embrace change. By doing so, you'll not only navigate the complexities of your current market but also future-proof your business for challenges and opportunities yet to come.

Adapting to Market Changes

In the ever-evolving landscape of business, adapting to market changes isn't just a survival strategy – it's a thriving strategy. Imagine your business as a ship navigating through unpredictable waters. The seas can be calm and then get turbulent in the blink of an eye. This is the reality of markets. They fluctuate, customer preferences shift, new competitors emerge, and technological advancements force you to rethink your strategies. So, how do you stay ahead? How do you ensure your business isn't left in the dust? The answer lies in embracing change, not resisting it.

For starters, let's talk about the importance of agility. Agility in business means being able to move quickly and easily, adapting to changes as they come. This isn't just about having a nimble team; it's about creating an organizational culture that welcomes change. Encourage your team to view challenges as opportunities for growth. Foster an environment where innovation thrives, and employees feel empowered to experiment without fear of failure. After all, some of the best ideas come from taking risks and stepping outside comfort zones.

One effective approach to staying adaptable is through continuous market research. This isn't a one-time ordeal; it's an ongoing process. Use a variety of tools to keep tabs on industry trends, customer behaviors, and competitor strategies. From Google Trends to social media listening tools like Hootsuite, there are plenty of resources at your disposal. Regularly analyze this data and be prepared to pivot your strategies as needed. For example, if you notice a growing demand for eco-friendly products in your market, think about how you can tweak your offerings or marketing messages to align with this trend.

Another critical aspect of adapting to market changes is staying technologically adept. We've all seen how technology can disrupt entire industries overnight. Look at what Netflix did to Blockbuster or what Amazon has done to retail. Embrace new technologies that can give your business a competitive edge. This might mean investing in artificial intelligence to better understand customer needs or leveraging automation to streamline operations. The key is to be proactive in seeking out and implementing these technological advancements before your competitors do.

Flexibility also extends to your product or service offerings. Don't become so attached to your current lineup that you ignore demand shifts. If there's one constant in business, it's that customer preferences will continue to evolve. Keep your product or service portfolio diversified to better absorb these changes. Think about trialing new products on a smaller scale to gauge customer interest before a full-blown launch. This can be a cost-effective way to remain competitive and stay relevant.

Communication is another cornerstone in the realm of adaptability. Keep the lines of communication open with your customers, stakeholders, and even your competitors. Feedback is golden. It offers insights into what you're doing right and where there's room for improvement. Use surveys, social media interactions, and customer reviews to gather actionable feedback and adjust accordingly. Create a loop where feedback leads to change, and change leads to growth.

Moreover, financial agility cannot be overlooked. Maintain a flexible budget that allows you to reallocate resources swiftly in response to market changes. This might mean scaling back on certain initiatives that are no longer yielding results and investing more in areas showing promise. Keep a close eye on your financial health and use metrics to guide your decisions.

Let's not forget about the importance of a robust crisis management strategy. The market can be unpredictable. There could be economic downturns, supply chain disruptions, or unforeseen events like a global pandemic. A well-prepared business not only survives but can emerge stronger from crises. Develop a crisis management plan that outlines potential risks, response strategies, and communication plans. Regularly review and update this plan as your business grows and the market evolves.

There's also immense value in building strategic partnerships. Collaborate with others who can help you navigate market changes. These could be partnerships with other businesses, industry experts, or influencers. Collaborations bring fresh perspectives and new opportunities. They can also provide mutual support during turbulent times. Be open to forming alliances that can bolster your business resilience and adaptability.

Adopting a mindset of continual learning is crucial. Encourage yourself and your team to continually seek new knowledge, whether through formal education, reading industry reports, or attending webinars and conferences. The marketplace is a dynamic environment, and understanding the latest trends, tools, and theories can provide you with the foresight to anticipate changes before they occur.

In essence, adaptability should become second nature. It's not about being reactive but being proactive. An anticipatory stance allows you to foresee potential disruptions and prepare for them in advance. Instead of waiting for change to knock at your door, invite it in and make it work for you.

Wrapping it all up, your ability to adapt to market changes hinges on many factors: a proactive approach towards change, continuous market research, technological adeptness, diversified product offerings, robust communication channels, financial flexibility, a solid crisis management plan, strategic partnerships, and a commitment to ongoing learning. It's about creating a vision where change is not seen as a threat but as a gateway to new possibilities and greater success.

Remember, the businesses that thrive are the ones that don't get comfortable standing still. They're constantly moving, evolving, and striving to become better than they were yesterday. So, embrace change, adapt swiftly, and keep your eyes on your long-term vision.

Chapter 25: Preparing For Exits

As your journey approaches its peak, it's crucial to start thinking about your exit strategy. Whether you're considering selling your business or taking it public, evaluating all possible exit strategies helps ensure you make an informed decision that aligns with your long-term goals. Begin by having detailed financial records and growth forecasts ready, as potential buyers or investors will scrutinize these. It's also wise to enhance your business operations and showcase scalability. This not only increases your business's appeal but can also significantly boost its valuation. Prepare yourself mentally and emotionally for the transition, understanding that stepping away from your creation might be challenging. Engage with advisors and mentors who can walk you through the nuances of a sale or IPO, ensuring you're well-equipped for every step of the process. While the exit might mark the end of one chapter, it's just the beginning of new opportunities and endeavors.

Evaluating Exit Strategies

Alright, folks, you've built up your business to the point that you're thinking about making an exit. Congratulations! That's not a small feat. Evaluating exit strategies is a pivotal move, requiring the same meticulous planning and thoughtful consideration you put into starting and growing your business. Whether you're ready to cash out or preparing for the future, choosing the right exit strategy is crucial.

First off, let's talk options. The most common exit strategies include selling your business, merging with another company, or going public through an Initial Public Offering (IPO). Each of these avenues has its distinct advantages and potential pitfalls. They're akin to choosing between different routes on a map where each path will offer different scenery, challenges, and final destinations.

Selling your business outright could be the quickest and most straightforward way to realize your entrepreneurial efforts' value. If you're leaning towards a sale, keep in mind the variety of buyers who might be interested. You have strategic buyers looking to enhance their current business portfolio and financial buyers such as private equity firms out to make a solid return on investment. And then there are individual buyers who might be looking to operate the business themselves. Each type requires a different approach and garners varying valuations.

Businesses with a strong brand, stable revenue, and growth prospects can fetch top dollar. Plan accordingly. Preparing beforehand with a detailed audit of operations, customer base, contracts, and intellectual property can immensely bolster your valuation. Think of it like staging a house for sale; you want to present the best version of your business.

Now, merging with another company is another strategic exit that allows you to partner up for potentially great mutual benefit. It's not merely an end but an evolution. Mergers often involve a combination of businesses that offer complementary strengths, services, or products. This can make your combined entity a stronger competitor in the marketplace, potentially higher than the sum of its parts.

However, the merger route requires intricate negotiations. You'll need to consider corporate culture, operational strategies, and future growth plans. Due diligence from both parties can make or break the deal. It's akin to entering into a partnership or marriage, where compatibility and mutual objectives need to align. Misalignment could lead to chaos rather than growth.

Then there's the glamorous yet daunting route of going public with an IPO. Taking this path means opening your company to public investors, which can significantly raise funds and enhance your brand's reputation. But it also comes with regulatory scrutiny and the need for transparent operations and disclosures.

Another exit strategy is passing the business on to a family member or a trusted employee. This is more common in family-owned businesses and could be less disruptive than selling or merging. This route preserves the legacy you've built and ensures it stays within trusted hands. However, this option requires grooming the next generation of leadership, which isn't a process that happens overnight.

In considering any of these paths, timing is everything. Market conditions, your business's life stage, and your personal readiness all play into the equation. Selling in a booming economy when your business metrics are glowing can maximize returns. On the flip side, a hastily planned exit in turbulent times might result in a lower valuation or stricter terms.

Before making any decisions, weigh your personal goals and the company's objectives. Do you want to retire peacefully, fund another venture, or ensure the brand and mission you've built continue to thrive? Your answers to these questions can guide which strategy is most suitable.

It's vital to consult with professionals – accountants, lawyers, and advisors – familiar with exit strategies. They can provide you with valuable insights into tax implications, legal hurdles, and potential hidden pitfalls. Just as you wouldn't DIY brain surgery, don't go it alone here.

Another angle to consider is your team. An exit can be as disconcerting for them as it is exciting for you. Transparent communication can help manage expectations and alleviate anxiety. Whether it's about retaining talent post-sale or ensuring fair severance, consider how your exit strategy impacts the people who helped build your dream into reality.

Ultimately, evaluating exit strategies isn't a one-size-fits-all endeavor. It's about balancing your financial goals, considering your legacy, and ensuring the future success of the enterprise you've nurtured from inception. The right exit strategy will not only provide you with financial windfall but can also set the stage for your next big adventure. Because, in all likelihood, this isn't the end of your entrepreneurial journey – it's just the beginning of a new chapter.

Preparing for Sale or IPO

So, the day is finally in sight – you're considering either selling your business or taking it public. This isn't just another brick in the wall; it's the pinnacle of the entrepreneurial journey. Preparing for a sale or an Initial Public Offering (IPO) is like getting ready for the ultimate grand finale. You want to ensure that your business is a lean, mean machine poised for a smooth transition. Whether you're looking to hand over the keys to another driver or invite the public to hop on board, the process demands meticulous preparation and strategic foresight.

First things first, ensure your financials are in tip-top shape. Prospective buyers and investors will scrutinize every number, so you don't want any fiscal skeletons in the closet. Start by conducting thorough audits and ensure your books are clean and transparent. This is where your financial management efforts from Chapter 11 will really pay off. Engaging a professional CPA can be immensely beneficial; they'll provide that objective perspective to ensure everything adds up. Transparency is king, and clear, accurate financial statements are your crown jewels.

Having your financials in order is just one piece of the puzzle. You also need to get your legal affairs squared away. Legal due diligence will be exhaustive, covering every aspect from intellectual property to employee contracts. Make sure all your documentation is easily accessible and well-organized. Engage with legal professionals to conduct a mock due diligence process, identifying and mitigating any potential red flags. This will save you time, headaches, and potentially lost deals down the line.

A potential buyer or investor will also be deeply interested in your customer base and market position. Ensure your customer data is robust and clearly presented. This means detailed analytics on customer acquisition costs, lifetime value, churn rates, and other key metrics discussed in Chapter 17. Essentially, you want to showcase a solid, loyal customer base that promises growth and profitability.

Don't downplay the power of your brand. Having a strong, consistent brand pulls a lot of weight. Review your brand messaging (Chapter 16) and make

CHAPTER 25: PREPARING FOR EXITS

sure it aligns with your long-term vision. Whether you're selling or going public, a well-crafted brand story can significantly boost perceived value. Companies with strong brands are more attractive to both buyers and public investors because they indicate not just current success, but future growth potential.

Next, systematization is essential. Investors want to see a business that can run like a well-oiled machine without the founder's constant involvement. By now, you should have streamlined operations (Chapter 6), automated various aspects of your business (Chapter 14), and outsourced tasks effectively. Your goal is to show a prospective buyer or investor that the business can continue thriving, even if you're no longer at the helm.

Employee morale and company culture also play a crucial role. Teams that are motivated and productive add considerable value. Make sure to communicate the strength of your company's culture and the talent of your team. This could mean creating an employee handbook, showcasing testimonials from team members, or demonstrating low turnover rates. Happy employees are the backbone of a resilient business.

It's also worth noting the importance of demonstrating growth potential. Always have a business plan for the next few years, showing new markets you can tap into, potential product line expansions, and avenues for scaling. Just because you've hit your milestones doesn't mean the journey ends here. An attractive growth strategy makes your business more enticing and adds several zeroes to your valuation.

Regarding operational efficiency, pay close attention to supply chain readiness. Your supply chain strategies from Chapter 6 and inventory management techniques need to be sharp. Prospective buyers or investors will want to know that you can meet demand efficiently and cost-effectively. Highlight any relationships with key suppliers and detail how you've optimized your supply chain for maximum efficiency and minimum delay.

Now, let's talk about valuation. Understanding how much your business is worth isn't just about sticking a finger in the air. It involves serious number crunching and often, the help of business valuation experts. There are various methods to consider – from discounted cash flow analysis to comparable company analysis. Knowing your worth ensures you don't leave money on the table and positions you strongly in negotiations.

Speaking of negotiations, the art of the deal can't be underestimated. Always have a negotiation strategy in place. Consider potential deal structures, whether it's an all-cash deal, stock options, or a combination of both. Prepare mentally and practically for these conversations; role-playing scenarios can be surprisingly effective. Always remember, the aim is a win-win – when both parties feel good about the deal, it's more likely to succeed in the long run.

When aiming for an IPO, things get a bit more intricate. Firstly, you'll need to pick an underwriter – an investment bank that will buy shares in your company and sell them to the public. This step involves heavy due diligence, roadshows to pitch to potential investors, and finally, pricing the IPO. It's a long, involved process and something you'll likely want a specialized team to handle.

Your public image will also play a bigger role when preparing for an IPO. It's essential to have a solid public relations strategy in place. You'll need to tell a compelling story not just to investors, but to the world. Media presence, positive press coverage, and a strong social media presence all become critical components of your strategy.

Review your tech stack and intellectual property. Ensure that any proprietary technology is well-protected with patents or trademarks. Potential buyers or public investors will want to see a moat around your business that prevents competitors from easily replicating your success. This is where the insights from Chapter 23 on Intellectual Property Protection come in handy.

Lastly, consider how you'll transition out of a leadership role if that's part of the plan. Succession planning ensures that the business doesn't falter once you're gone. Identify key players within your organization who can take on more significant roles and ensure they are prepared. If you're maintaining a stake in the company post-sale or IPO, be clear about your future involvement.

In summary, preparing for a sale or IPO isn't a walk in the park, but with meticulous preparation, it can be a rewarding capstone to your entrepreneurial journey. Nail your financials, legal documentation, customer data, and brand identity. Ensure your business operations are efficient, and your team is motivated. Chart out a clear growth strategy, get an accurate valuation, negotiate smartly, and make sure your transition plan is solid. This is the grand finale, where all the hard work pays off, opening new chapters for you and your business. Let's make it a standing ovation-worthy performance.

Conclusion

As we wrap up this uncharted journey to your first $1 million, it's time to reflect on how far you've come and look ahead to what the future holds. This one-year plan has walked you through every stage, from laying the groundwork to mastering advanced strategies. It's not just about hitting that seven-figure milestone; it's about evolving into a savvy, resilient entrepreneur capable of navigating the highs and lows of business life.

The essence of this journey boils down to executing with purpose and precision. You have identified your "why," conducted thorough market research, and narrowed down a winning product idea. You've gone from bootstrapping to potentially attracting investors, and you've successfully launched your product into the world. These foundational elements aren't just stepping stones to success—they're the bedrock on which your entire entrepreneurial venture stands.

We've emphasized the importance of finding your target customers and crafting an irresistible offer. The initial months, often the most grueling, require grit and tenacity. But the reward is evident as you secure your first few sales and begin to build momentum. It's these early victories that set the stage for continuous growth.

When it comes to scaling, streamlining operations, and managing finances, efficiency is key. Adopting lean practices not only conserves resources but also amplifies profitability. Building systems around inventory management and customer experience prepares you for the explosive growth that follows. Remember, scalability isn't just about selling more; it's about maintaining quality and customer satisfaction as you grow.

CONCLUSION

From creating urgency to leveraging early adopters, your initial sales tactics will morph as you refine your approach. It's a dynamic process, constantly informed by data and customer feedback. Being adaptable and responsive to these insights leads to more effective and efficient marketing strategies. And don't forget the power of budget-conscious advertising and innovative marketing techniques to propel your business into the next phase.

Achieving a steady stream of sales requires optimizing conversion rates and deploying retargeting strategies. Integrating social media marketing and influencer partnerships expands your reach, bringing your product into the daily conversations of potential customers. These combined efforts help establish a strong foothold in the market and build a devoted customer base.

Customer loyalty remains a pivotal focus. It's not just about making one-time sales but forging lasting relationships. Implementing feedback loops and enhancing customer experience can turn satisfied buyers into brand advocates. The journey from 25 to 100 sales per day involves operational efficiencies and customer-centric innovations that keep clients coming back.

The tactical phase involves more than just sales growth; it's about financial stewardship. Managing your budget wisely and maintaining a healthy cash flow ensure that your business remains robust and resilient. Financial management isn't just about spreadsheets and balance sheets; it's about strategic planning that supports sustainable growth.

The final months of this one-year plan emphasize diversification and innovation. By establishing a product series and broadening your offerings, you create multiple revenue streams that fortify your business against market fluctuations. Automation and outsourcing further streamline operations, freeing your time to focus on strategic decisions and long-term goals.

Brand building and advanced marketing strategies solidify your market presence. Beyond mere transactions, it's about establishing a narrative that resonates with your audience. Consistent brand messaging fosters a sense of trust and loyalty, making customers feel part of your journey.

Constantly analyzing metrics and making data-driven decisions ensure that you're always on the pulse of your business. Key Performance Indicators (KPIs) and iterative testing are not just routine checks but integral parts of your growth strategy. They inform you of what's working, what needs adjustment, and where untapped opportunities lie.

Profit optimization strategies, such as reducing costs and increasing average order value, further propel your financial health. Continuous improvement isn't an endpoint but an ongoing process of learning, adapting, and innovating. Your ability to implement feedback and pivot when necessary keeps you relevant and resilient in an ever-changing market landscape.

We've also touched on less glamorous but equally critical aspects like crisis management and legal compliance. Navigating downturns, handling negative feedback, and understanding regulatory requirements are all part of the entrepreneurial journey. They prepare you to face challenges head-on and emerge stronger.

Finally, as you achieve your milestones, planning for the long-term sustainability of your business becomes paramount. Building a community, fostering networking opportunities, and seeking mentorship not only enrich your entrepreneurial journey but also lay the groundwork for future ventures. Evaluating exit strategies like a sale or IPO provides options for future transitions, ensuring that you're prepared for whatever comes next.

This one-year journey is not just a blueprint for reaching $1 million but a holistic guide to becoming the entrepreneur you aspire to be. The lessons learned, the challenges overcome, and the victories celebrated are all part of a larger narrative. It's your narrative. Armed with these insights, strategies, and the unwavering belief in your vision, you're not just reaching for financial milestones—you're building a legacy.

Appendix

Appendix A: Appendix

This appendix is crafted to be a treasure trove of additional resources, references, and tools that will help you on your entrepreneurial journey. Think of it as your secret weapon, packed with insights and information that can turn obstacles into opportunities and challenges into successes. Here you'll find a range of materials designed to complement the chapters of this book and provide actionable steps to accelerate your journey to your first $1 million.

Resource List

The journey to your first $1 million is exciting but can also feel overwhelming at times. To help you navigate this path, we've compiled a comprehensive list of resources that will guide you through various aspects of building and growing your business. This resource list is your go-to toolkit, filled with books, websites, tools, and services designed to give you an edge.

Books:

- *"The Lean Startup" by Eric Ries* – An invaluable guide on how to build a startup using lean methodology, making it easier to innovate and adapt quickly.
- *"Zero to One" by Peter Thiel* – A deep dive into creating unique products that can change the market.

- *"Good to Great" by Jim Collins* — Explores why some companies make the leap to greatness and others don't.

Websites and Online Communities:

- *Entrepreneur.com* — Offers articles, videos, and tools for entrepreneurs at all stages of their journey.
- *Reddit - r/Entrepreneur* — A community where you can ask questions and share insights with fellow entrepreneurs.
- *Startup Grind* — A global community of startups, founders, innovators, and creators.

Podcasts:

- *The Tim Ferriss Show* — Tim Ferriss interviews top performers to uncover their keys to success.
- *How I Built This* — Guy Raz interviews entrepreneurs and innovators about how they built their companies.
- *Smart Passive Income* — Pat Flynn shares his insights on building passive income streams and online businesses.

Market Research Tools:

- *Google Trends* — Offers insights into search trends and consumer interest over time.
- *Ahrefs* — Comprehensive tool for keyword research, backlink analysis, and competitive analysis.
- *SurveyMonkey* — Easy-to-use survey tool for gathering consumer feedback and conducting market research.

Funding Resources:

- *AngelList* — Connect with angel investors and venture capitalists looking

to invest in startups.
- *Kickstarter* – A crowdfunding platform that allows you to raise money from backers for creative projects.
- *SBA (Small Business Administration)* – Offers loans, grants, and other financial assistance to small businesses.

Sales and Marketing Tools:

- *HubSpot* – A powerful CRM system that includes inbound marketing, sales, and customer service tools.
- *Mailchimp* – An email marketing service to manage mailing lists and create email campaigns.
- *Canva* – Easy-to-use graphic design tool for creating eye-catching marketing materials.

Operational Tools:

- *Trello* – A project management tool that helps teams collaborate and manage tasks efficiently.
- *Slack* – A team communication platform that streamlines communication and collaboration.
- *QuickBooks* – Accounting software tailored for small businesses, helping you manage finances with ease.

Customer Experience Tools:

- *Zendesk* – A customer service platform that provides omnichannel support and improves customer satisfaction.
- *Hootsuite* – Manages your social media presence, schedules posts, and provides analytics.
- *Trustpilot* – Collect customer reviews and feedback, building trust with potential customers.

These resources are designed to provide you with a wealth of knowledge, tools, and services that will support you throughout your entrepreneurial journey. Reading books, participating in online communities, listening to podcasts, and leveraging various tools can help you develop the skills and knowledge necessary to overcome challenges and seize opportunities.

While this list is extensive, it's by no means exhaustive. The world of business is ever-evolving, and new tools and resources are constantly emerging. Stay curious and keep exploring new ways to grow your business. Continuously updating your knowledge and skills will keep you ahead of the curve and prepared for whatever comes your way.

Remember, leveraging these resources effectively requires a proactive mindset. Don't just read the books or listen to the podcasts—apply what you learn. Engage actively in online communities, try out different tools, and see what works best for your business.

Lastly, never underestimate the power of mentorship and networking. Use platforms like LinkedIn, attend industry conferences, and engage with local business communities. Building relationships with mentors and peers can provide invaluable insights and open doors to opportunities you may not have anticipated.

Make this resource list your starting point. Embark on your journey with confidence, and use these tools as your guideposts. Your path to $1 million won't be a straight line, but with the right resources, you'll navigate the twists and turns more effectively.

Your entrepreneurial journey is unique, and the resources you choose to rely on will play a significant role in your success. Keep this list close, refer to it often, and don't be afraid to explore new avenues. Good luck!

Glossary

Understanding the key terms and concepts in your journey to the first $1 million is crucial. Here, we've compiled a glossary to help you grasp the essential terms used throughout this book.

- **Bootstrapping** – Starting a business with minimal financial resources, relying on personal savings and self-generated funds from initial sales.
- **Burn Rate** – The rate at which a company spends its cash reserves or capital.
- **Cash Flow** – The total amount of money being transferred into and out of a business, especially affecting liquidity.
- **Conversion Rate** – The percentage of visitors to your website or audience who take a desired action, such as making a purchase.
- **Customer Acquisition Cost (CAC)** – The cost associated with convincing a consumer to buy your product or service, including marketing and sales expenses.
- **Influencer Partnerships** – Collaborations with influencers who promote your product to their audience in exchange for compensation or free products.
- **Intellectual Property (IP)** – Creations of the mind for which exclusive rights are recognized (e.g., patents, trademarks, and copyrights).
- **Key Performance Indicators (KPIs)** – Quantifiable measures that gauge the performance of various aspects of a business, helping to determine the effectiveness of strategies and operations.
- **Market Research** – The process of gathering, analyzing, and interpreting information about a market, including information about the target market and consumers.
- **Product-Market Fit** – The degree to which a product satisfies a strong market demand, often a key milestone for startups.
- **Return on Investment (ROI)** – A performance measure used to evaluate the efficiency or profitability of an investment.
- **Retargeting** – Online advertising strategy that targets consumers who have previously visited your website or engaged with your brand.
- **Scaling** – Expanding a business smoothly by managing increased demands and boosting production or sales while minimizing costs.
- **Supply Chain Management** – The management of the flow of goods and services, involving the movement and storage of raw materials, inventory, and finished products.

This glossary will be your quick reference guide throughout the book. When you encounter a term that's unclear, return here for a clear definition.

Further Reading

In your quest towards reaching your first $1 million, understanding and mastering business terminology is only the starting point. Terms like "cash flow," "scalability," and "market research" become vital components in your entrepreneurial toolkit. While the Glossary gives you a foundational understanding, it's only the beginning. Further reading will provide deeper insights, context, and applications that transform jargon into actionable strategies.

First, consider diving into foundational business books that expand on these terms with real-world applications and case studies. Books like "The Lean Startup" by Eric Ries and "Zero to One" by Peter Thiel take you through the nuts and bolts of building a business from scratch. These books help bridge the gap between understanding terminology and implementing it effectively in your business strategy. They're filled with examples that show how successful companies navigated their challenges, something that can be incredibly inspiring and instructional for you.

Next, explore academic journals and papers focused on entrepreneurship and business management. Publications like the Harvard Business Review and MIT Sloan Management Review offer in-depth articles on the latest trends, case studies, and empirical research. While they may seem dense, these resources provide valuable insights into how businesses thrive or fail, offering lessons that can be directly applied to your own enterprise.

Don't underestimate the power of blogs and podcasts either. Entrepreneurs like Tim Ferriss and Gary Vaynerchuk offer practical advice and personal anecdotes that make complex business concepts more accessible. In their podcasts, topics such as "scaling up," "digital marketing," and "customer acquisition" are explored in a conversational, easy-to-understand manner. It's like having a mentor in your ear, guiding you through the intricacies of building a sustainable business.

APPENDIX

For those who prefer a more visual learning style, YouTube channels dedicated to entrepreneurs offer an abundance of content. Channels such as Y Combinator and Skillshare provide tutorials and real-life case studies from successful startups. This visual approach can be particularly helpful when trying to grasp more abstract concepts like customer journey mapping or lean methodologies.

Online courses are another invaluable resource. Platforms like Coursera, edX, and Udemy offer courses focused on various aspects of entrepreneurship—from finance and marketing to operations and innovation. Many of these courses are created by top-tier universities and industry experts, giving you access to world-class education right at your fingertips. Look for courses that offer practical assignments and real-life case studies, as these will help solidify your understanding and give you hands-on experience.

For a more interactive learning experience, consider joining entrepreneurial forums and social media groups. Platforms like Reddit, LinkedIn, and specialized business forums allow you to engage with other entrepreneurs, ask questions, and share experiences. These communities often share articles, resources, and advice that can help you navigate the labyrinthine world of business ownership.

Let's not forget the power of mentorship. Mentors can provide personalized advice tailored to your unique situation. They've been through the wringer and can offer guidance on specific challenges you're facing. Books like "Tools of Titans" by Tim Ferriss compile wisdom from various industry leaders, offering bite-sized advice that can be immediately implemented. This can be a great complement to having a personal mentor.

Now, let's talk about industry-specific literature. Depending on the industry you're entering, there will be specialized publications that offer deeper insights. For instance, if you're diving into tech, books like "The Innovator's Dilemma" by Clayton Christensen are essential reads. For retail, "Delivering Happiness" by Tony Hsieh offers invaluable insights into customer experience and company culture.

Furthermore, government and non-profit organizations often publish white papers and guides on small business operations and entrepreneurship.

The Small Business Administration (SBA) website, for example, offers a plethora of resources, templates, and guides to help you navigate various aspects of running a business—from writing a business plan to securing funds and managing operations.

To stay updated with the latest trends and innovations, subscribe to newsletters from reputable business analysts and consultancy firms like McKinsey, Deloitte, and PwC. These organizations consistently publish articles that offer forward-looking perspectives on market trends, consumer behavior, and disruptive technologies. Staying updated with these can provide you with a competitive edge, helping you to anticipate changes and adapt your strategies accordingly.

Lastly, never stop experimenting and learning from your own experiences. Your business is a living entity that will evolve over time. Keep a journal of your strategies, outcomes, and lessons learned. This not only helps you reflect and improve but also serves as a valuable resource you can refer back to during challenging times.

At the end of the day, further reading is about building a comprehensive knowledge base that empowers you to make informed decisions. It's not just about accumulating information but understanding how to apply that knowledge in real-world scenarios. So keep reading, keep learning, and keep pushing forward. Every piece of information you absorb brings you one step closer to that first $1 million.

www.ingramcontent.com/pod-product-compliance
Lightning Source LLC
Chambersburg PA
CBHW071455220526
45472CB00003B/807